THE
GMILLIONAIRES
ENIU S

*Helen
d a Card
Make a Difference*

Dream Big Dreams

I Believe In You!

Super Dave

Published 2007
LIFESUCCESS PUBLISHING, LLC
8900 E Pinnacle Peak Road, Suite D240
Scottsdale, AZ 85255

Telephone: 800.473.7134
Fax: 480.661.1014

E-mail: admin@lifesuccesspublishing.com
ISBN: 1-59930-011-5
Cover: LifeSuccess Publishing
Layout: Lloyd Arbour & LifeSuccess Publishing

COMPANIES, ORGANIZATIONS, INSTITUTIONS, AND INDUSTRY
PUBLICATIONS: Quantity discounts are available on bulk purchases of this book
for reselling, educational purposes, subscription incentives, gifts, sponsorship,
or fundraising. Special books or book excerpts can also be created to fit specific
needs such as private labeling with your logo on the cover and a message from a VIP
printed inside. For more information please contact our Special Sales Department at
LifeSuccess Publishing.

THE
G MILLIONAIRES
ENIU

HOW TO WAKE UP THE MONEY MAGIC WITHIN YOU.

— DAVID OGUNNAIKE —

~ *Dedication* ~

This book is dedicated to all those people who dream about having more, doing more and being more.

~ *Acknowledgments* ~

I would like to acknowledge all my teachers over the years. These include Bob Proctor, Gerry Robert, Tony Robbins, Zig Ziglar, and so many more. From them I have learned that I can accomplish anything if I keep my mind looking forward and keep learning and growing. Their contributions have changed my world.

I owe huge thanks to my immediate family - my dad, Engineer O.T. Ogunnaike, my mom, Denise Manning, both my sisters and their husbands, Susanna & Jason, and Rachelle & Fred, and of course my Super Brother, Phenomenal Patrick, along with my nephews, Juwon and Ryker, and my nieces, Mikaela, Jada and Aria, for all their support over the years.

I also want to thank my current and past friends, especially those who made a direct and positive impact in my life: Raymond and Kate Yee, Kosta and Deva Gharagozloo, Karim Premji, Milan Choulik, Empress Niambi, Hyacinth Smith, Poonam Jain, Tim and Margaret Kydd, Natasha Soogrim, Harabi Jamal, Robert and Violetta Borowski, Juanita Wright, Camille Clark, Piero Mbayo, Aki and Annette Vais, Sean and Alexa Murphy, Sonia Ahmed, Ernie and Carol Lafontaine, Allan and Eve Marston, Glenn and Connie Embleton, Desmond Palmer, Eric Eaton, Sirin Banu Patel, Jean Magill, Mohamed and Pam Premji, Zahid and Muhammad Ali, Ola Adedugbe, Kemi and Bayo Gasper, Joanna Dumitrascu, Kim Jason, Jack and Louise Zobell, Cynthia Mendoza, Julie Chisholm, Kunal and Pooja Khanna, Tom and Alma Burant, Debbie L. Hudson, Steve and Monique Briand, Phebe Trotman, Ramin Mesgarlou, Suzanne Robinson, Gabe and Nira Nave, Rana Khaled, my extended family, the countless new friends and acquaintances and all the associates that are part of The One Dream Team. You are all amazing people. Thank you all for being a part of my life.

I have to make special mention of three unique individuals who had the vision to create opportunities with companies that have allowed me to LIVE MY DREAMS, Michael Ellison for my Health, Gary Calhoun for my Wealth and Kody Bateman for my Mission. Thanks to you all, we are "Transforming Lives, One Person at a Time."

I would also like to thank all the people at LifeSuccess Publishing for their support. Working with Kandi Miller has been simply awesome, and the creative department is superb at doing their job. The post-production support is wonderful, especially the video production work done by Andrew Hunter and his team. Erin Woodward's management of this book, including her work with the editorial staff, has made this project a joy from start to finish.

How many times have you picked up a book just like this one and hoped it could change your life? I used to do exactly the same thing. A few short years ago I felt crushed by a mountain of debt, failed attempts at business, and an overwhelming sense of fear. I couldn't figure out why some people seemed to make money so easily but it was still a struggle for me.

During those dark days of my life I was fortunate enough to meet some wonderful people who also happened to be millionaires. They were patient and taught me what they knew. Using my new skills, my bank account went from $1.37 to more than $1 million in twenty-six months! The most important thing I learned was that it's not about the money. It's about me.

What I will share with you here is not some big secret or scheme, or about being in any particular type of business. It's about starting where you are, with what you have. Within the pages of this book you will learn how to:

- Dispel the demons of regret, indecision, and fear
- Set achievable goals
- Dream big (and reach those dreams!)
- Master the power of a positive attitude
- Let go of the past and start over
- Use the law of attraction

This is not a book for people who merely want more money. This is a book for those who want to transform their lives – and it can happen for you, too. Let me show you the secret of awakening your own Millionaire Genius.

~ David Ogunnaike ~

∾ *Foreword* ∾
by Bob Proctor

If you have ever wanted to have a *Millionaire Mindset*, you'll love this book. David Ogunnaike shows you how to make money, plain and simple. If you want to generate a new life for yourself, your family, your organization, your sales team, or your company, you'll love this book.

David empowers people who know very little about using the power of the mind and thinking to create the financial abundance they desire, including free time. By the end of this book you should be armed with much more than you bargained for. You will see how your conditioning has created the life you have and exactly how to change it forever. This book contains sound advice on how you can wake up the Money Magic within YOU.

One warning, though: If you are looking for a "Get Rich Quick" book, this one is probably not for you. Somehow, Super Dave (as he is often referred to) has avoided all the typical psycho-babble of books promising huge windfalls without changing your paradigms in any way. In this book you will get practical strategies that work to produce lasting changes.

I loved this book. It has a major role to play for those of us who have neither the time nor the inclination to delve into massive tomes on psychology, motivation and self-awareness.

This book gives you the bottom line on how to improve your life.

It is, indeed, a sure winner!

~ Bob Proctor ~
Bestselling Author of *You Were Born Rich*
(www.bobproctor.com)

XII

~ *Table of Contents* ~

> *"If you are going to win a battle, you must ensure that the mind controls the body. Never the other way around."*
>
> ~ General George S. Patton ~

~ *Introduction* ~

SUPER CHARGE YOUR LIFE

I come from humble beginnings. I am probably the least likely person to be writing a book such as this, but I learned years ago that to win big in life one needs to find excellent mentors and to practice their advice.

I was born July 8th, 1971, in Ottawa, Canada. My father is Nigerian and my mother is French Canadian. I guess from early childhood, without really realizing it, I was learning about overcoming challenges. My mom was willing to work through challenges like getting married to someone from a totally different continent and culture. It wasn't easy for her, but the long-term benefit of having a family made it worth the problems she faced. In 1974, after my mom finished her degree at Carlton University and my dad received his Engineering degree at the University of Ottawa, our whole family (I also had two sisters by then) moved to Nigeria. My brother was born there in 1977, and that's where we grew up. I learned my English there and just had a great time. You have to remember, we made do with what we had where we were because we didn't know there was anything better.

People ask me, "Dave, have you always been this positive?" and my answer is always, "Yes!" Things weren't always perfect, but I was brought up in a loving family household. I *always* knew that my dad and mom loved me and I never doubted it; but something odd happened while we grew up in Nigeria. Because we children are of mixed race (Mom is white, Dad is black), we were referred to as "Oyibo," the common term for all white people in Nigeria. Whether we were walking down the street or driving in a car, it didn't matter, anywhere we showed up, everyone around was sure to be aware of it. Adults and kids of all ages would run up to us and start yelling, "Oyibo." My mom really didn't like it, but I thought it was great and I would just wave in return. I grew up thinking I was a celebrity.

While growing up in Nigeria I got special treatment both in school and just generally in life because we were "Oyibos." For example, when the whole class was getting punished for something, I would be excluded. When they needed someone to be class leader, I would be chosen. And so on. It was great.

All this just reinforced in me that I'm unique.

In August of 1985 we moved back to Ottawa, Canada. It was getting pretty tough in Nigeria at that time, and our parents thought it would serve us better to go to school in Canada. There our schooling would be recognized around the world instead of in just one country. At least that is what we were told.

In Nigeria, there had never been any talk about money in the family. We weren't wealthy, but there wasn't anything we went without. My parents always provided for all of us.

My mom had been a teacher in Nigeria. When we arrived in Canada she wanted to work as a nurse, but she had to do a refresher course because she had been out of nursing for too long, and even though her degree was originally in nursing her training wasn't current. That meant she couldn't work until she got classified all over again. We stayed in my aunt's basement when we first arrived, and a month later we moved into an apartment.

We had to go on welfare for a year, and I remember getting clothes from my mom's friends and from the Salvation Army. Our beds were old mattresses that people had thrown out. Again, I think because of my excitement at being in a new country and the prospect of actually seeing snow I didn't really see any of this as depressing or as a bad situation.

Where things really started to affect me was in high school. When I started I was 5'3" and no one could understand what I was saying because my accent was so strong. I was always being asked to repeat myself, which caused me to feel conspicuous (but not in the "celebrity" way that I felt in Nigeria). On top of that there were only about eight "black" people in my whole school at that time.

I literally went from "white" to "black." Can you believe that? In Nigeria I had been called "Oyibo," but in Canada I was considered "colored." I wasn't treated as anyone special or unique, I was just like everyone else. I started ninth grade with no friends because I didn't come from eighth grade with the rest of my class. I made one friend in French class, Sam Gao, and in fact he was my only friend until twelfth grade.

So for me most of high school was just a blur. I played table tennis, badminton and was part of the Star Trek club. I liked girls but wouldn't speak to them because they couldn't understand what I was saying. My attitude became one of, "Why bother?" So I didn't.

It can be sad what we tell ourselves. It can be a lot worse if we act on it. The subconscious mind doesn't know any better.

After we moved to Canada my mom would often talk about how there wasn't enough money for this or that, and she had to work nights because those were the only shifts open to a new nurse.

The one thing I do remember is that I came to a decision: I would make sure that I would never have to worry about bills. And at the end of tenth grade when my classmates and I went around signing each other's yearbooks, a guy said that the way I signed my name looked like a Millionaire's signature. And I thought, "A Millionaire huh?… Hmmm….. A Millionaire wouldn't have to worry about bills. That's it! I'm going to become a MILLIONAIRE!"

It's amazing what can happen when you choose the right words to speak out. And what's more amazing is that you don't know when you'll say that one thing that can change the whole direction of someone's life.

Since eleventh grade I tried different businesses, because in my research I learned that's how people became millionaires - not through a JOB.

In fact, I heard that J.O.B. stood for Just Over Broke, and that left a deep impression on me.

In my quest to become a Millionaire all I did at first was rack up debts. You see, I never actually wanted a Million Dollars in my account, I just wanted to have enough money so that if I wanted to eat out, buy a shirt, give $10 to a homeless person, or pay a bill, I could do it without thinking about whether I could afford it.

I was reading the motivational books and going to different seminars. I wanted to learn the secret of what made people earn extraordinary incomes, how they became Millionaires. I learned that if you want something you have to find someone that has what you want, and then listen and do what they tell you to do. If you do then it stands to reason that you'll have what they have.

One morning I went to a breakfast meeting because I wanted to learn about other people's businesses, and when people were allowed to give their 1 minute advertising speech, one fellow stood up and said he had FREE tickets for a Creating Wealth Seminar where a Millionaire was going to be the speaker. All I heard was Millionaire and FREE, so I jumped up and said I wanted a ticket. Jack Nakamoto gave me the ticket, and I still carry that ticket with me today.

On June 21, 1999, I attended the Creating Wealth Seminar with my friend Harabi to listen to the best-selling author and speaker Gerry Robert. There must have been over 150 people there, but after his talk I just walked up to the front of the room, shook his hand and said, "You're a Millionaire and that's what I want to be. You tell me what do to, and I'll DO IT!" Since 1999, when I started DOING instead of just THINKING, I got more done, but things weren't all perfect. In fact I had more challenges.

In 2001 I moved to Toronto, Canada, because while in Ottawa I read a passage in Zig Ziglar's book, *Over the Top*. He said, "If you want to change your circumstances, you have to change where you are in life." I though that "change your circumstance" could mean either mentally or physically, so I chose physically and moved to a new city. Toronto. This time I was staying with my sister and sleeping in my nephew's room. At 6'5" I was trying to fit in the lower level of his bunk bed, which was made for eight-year olds. But I had adopted the attitude of, "I'll do whatever it takes to make a difference in my life," and I did it.

I started to have a couple of successes and took bigger risks, but with no real plan of action. So by 2003 I was almost $100,000 in debt from failed businesses, owing almost half on credit cards and loans co-signed by my mom.

In July 2003, I thought, "If I can't even take care of myself, how am I ever going to take care of a family, financially?" I had to make a choice: I would either continue playing around in life or get serious and look for some kind of business that I would learn, commit to and, once and for all, succeed at.

That was it, I was sick and tired of begin SICK AND TIRED. I had very little money saved up, $1.37 to be exact. But I was willing to put in the effort, the sweat equity. I just had to find the right type of business.

In November 2003 I was actively researching different Network Marketing Opportunities. In December 2003 I found a home-based business opportunity with a company that, together with my preparedness, strong work ethic and another $100 from my mom's credit card, enabled me to become debt free within six months. Twenty six months later I became a REAL MILLIONAIRE.

> **\mil-lion-aire\ (noun)** – wealthy person – somebody whose net worth or income is more than one million dollars.

People now ask me, "Super Dave how does it feel?" My response is always, "SUPER!"

What I love is the fact that I've played a role in changing people's financial lives for the better, and in return that has given me the Time and Money Freedom that I've always wanted. I smile everyday when I wake up. When I think back to everything that I went through, I wouldn't change a thing because it's all those things that prepared me to be where I am today. And you can do the same.

I have personally seen the power of acting on the positive recommendations and suggestions of others. An early mentor of mine was (and still is) Gerry Robert, author of *The Millionaire Mindset.* He showed me a few things about how my self-limiting beliefs were holding me back. I acted on his advice, and I have become the most successful leader in a company that has tens of thousands of people. How did I do it? I acted. I found the courage to take that first step, and that's what I hope this book will help you to do, too.

Why is it that when some people win the lottery they often go broke again within in a few short years? I truly believe one reason is that they never learned the secrets of thinking like a wealthy person. I constantly see people living their lives from paycheck to paycheck, struggling all the while and not changing anything. They are trying to figure out how to get out of the woods, always going in circles, listening to the wrong people, making poor choices over and over again. It seems that life is drudgery for them. On the other hand, I have seen people take hold of this knowledge and turn their lives around. Results change when people change their thinking. Indeed, I have seen ordinary people without business experience simply take off financially.

This is exactly what happened to me. I didn't win the lottery. I just woke up the Millionaire Genius within me. You can do the same. It may not be easy as we go along, and there will be times I am going to be blunt. I am going to do my best to cause you to think about things you've never thought of before. Just do me a favor; don't reject the idea. Realize that if you are going to go to a better place financially, you are going to have to change some things. And *doing* first requires thinking. If you change your *thinking*, your actions will change, and if you change your actions, the results are going to change.

Here's an example: In Africa the natives use an ingenious method for catching monkeys. They hollow out a coconut shell by cutting a small hole at one end. The hole is just large enough to allow a monkey's hand to fit through. In the hollowed shell they place a few peanuts. They tie the coconut shell to a strong, thick cord and wait in hiding for the monkey. When a monkey discovers the nuts inside the shell, he reaches in and grasps them in his fist. But the hole is too small to allow the tightly clenched fist to escape. At this moment the native pulls on the cord, and the monkey, who won't let go of those peanuts to save his life, is caught. Like these monkeys, too often we clench tightly to our own peanut ideas for fear that we may lose them, when all the while these are the very ideas that hold us captive and deny us the freedom we long for.

I am glad you decided to leave the past behind and look forward to a brighter future using your Millionaire Genius. There is going to be a lot of confrontation throughout this program, confrontation between your old programming and your new programming. You are in a battle. The battle will be against your old conditioning versus this new conditioning. I will make statements that will go directly against what you are conditioned to do, to think and to be. You are going to hear voices inside your head that are going to come from your old programming, voices that will disagree with what I am going to tell you in this book. All I am going to ask of you is to trust in the process. Through this system I'll give you the tools to make the mental shift you need to make to create wealth. You *can* have more of what you deserve in life. You *can* be the kind of person you want to be. You *can* go to the places you want to go, and you *can* go in style. And you can do it regardless of your old conditioning, or your friends, or maybe even what your own spouse thinks you can't do or what you should do instead.

Do *you* believe that you personally can become wealthy? That is the all-important question and the one that we will examine in depth. Most people find that they simply lack direction in their lives. They don't give any time to considering what they really want and merely accept what's sent their way. But don't you ever wonder if things could be different? The answer is, *yes they can be!* But you must first be willing to change your mind about *you.*

Have you ever sat down and thought about your life? No, I mean REALLY thought about your life? If you have, then you may have asked yourself, "How did I end up here?" Though each person has the opportunity to choose how he or she lives, many float through life on the path of least resistance - until one day they look back over what may be years of going with the flow only to realize they feel trapped. They are hemmed in by circumstances, living a life they hate and working at a job they hate even worse.

No one plans for a mediocre life, but many people end up with a mediocre life by not planning. Ask any poor senior citizen if he wrote out clear, measurable goals for his life when he was younger. We probably all know what the answer would be. Now, for contrast, ask a person who reaches the golden years without any financial worries how he got there. People who reach this period of life financially fit have probably developed and stuck with a plan that included goal-setting. Goal-setting is a major part of my system, and we will spend a large amount of time on it in this book.

We can do much more than we think. We have incredible resources, unlimited resources available to us. It would shock most people to know just how much they could achieve in life if they tried, or if they just used what they had available within them. Because most people do not understand how much potential they possess, they limit their aspirations to the improvements they know they can presently achieve. They can't perceive themselves in a better place or with a better life. I'll address this limiting thought process directly and give you tools to learn to change your thought patterns and visualize your new life.

Now, set your mind free and think: If you could have anything you wanted in life, what would it be? If you could do anything you wanted, or be whatever you wanted, what would you choose? You must want something to change in order for it to happen. I hope the fact that you picked up this book is proof of that desire. Don't limit your dreams to what you think you can have. You must give yourself a chance to dream and to risk. And as long as people accept limitation, they will not be motivated to discover the great opportunities that lie ahead of them.

You may have picked up a "change your life" type of book in the past, sat and read it and then thought, "Wow, that might work." But then, as the days and weeks pass, it gets pushed to the back of your mind and "reality" takes over.

In this book you will learn how to make these ideas and goals your reality. It's not just a system of instruction; it is a way to change your thinking about yourself, about money, and about what you can achieve. Once your mind is in the right mode to accept the changes you want, your life will become all you ever dreamed.

Now I realize that change is hard. Change takes time, and change can be scary. But it doesn't have to be that way. Each day when you get out of bed you have an active choice. You choose how you will respond to the trials and tribulations of everyday life; and yes, you also choose to succeed or merely go along for the ride.

I'm sure you are thinking that it's not easy to decide to choose a different path. But I will show you that it can be. Making the decision to change how you are perceived and deciding you want to seek out success is the hardest step. It's hard because you have to absolutely believe in your own ability.

Each person seems to be born with an internal self-belief barometer. Some are higher than others are, but with determination anyone can boost his confidence level and see his future become brighter each day. The trick is to turn off your internal critic. That is the one that says, "You've made too many mistakes, this is the best you'll ever get." Or, "You're not smart enough to succeed, you never went to college."

Ridiculous as it is, most people beat themselves up on a daily basis for what they can't or didn't do instead of focusing on the possibilities. They believe the lies they tell themselves and never envision a positive outcome to anything they try.

But it's not enough just to say, "I want to change." You need a plan, one that you can believe in and follow on your path to success. This book will show you step by step how you can change they way you are perceived and how to use that new perception to your advantage to increase your circle of influence.

CHAPTER ONE

SUPER ATTITUDE

CHAPTER ONE

Super Attitude

Sitting in the airport one day, I watched the rain streaming against the glass. I'd already been there two hours, and the gate agent just announced another delay due to weather. The horde of travelers let out a collective groan, but most resigned themselves to the situation. I walked to the book store and bought a well-known business book that I had been intending to read for at least six months and settled in for another wait.

When I returned, a woman on the same flight was standing at the counter screaming at the gate agent at the top of her lungs, "*I have* to get to Florida for this meeting. Millions of dollars is on the line!"

The gate agent apologized once again, motioning to the windows where the rain was now sheeting even heavier, interspersed with occasional flashes of thunder. The woman continued, "This is life or death! You *have* to do something!"

The woman continued to rant at the helpless gate agent for a few more minutes before finally giving up. It became clear to me that one of the defining character markers of every human being is how they respond to stress. The woman and I were both in the same situation, but she chose to completely lose control of her emotions and vent her negative tirade, while I made the best of it and read a great book.

Was I happy about the delay? No. Was there anything I could do about it? No. Did I want to get on a plane in the middle of a thunderstorm? Absolutely not! While we both took the same journey, I saw it as no big deal and a chance to do something positive with my time. I'm sure her version of events included how rotten the day was and how unhelpful the airline employees were. But that was her choice. Yes, I said "choice."

The moral of the story: How you live each day is not dictated by the circumstances of that day. It is dictated by how you handle those circumstances. You choose each morning to face the day with either a positive outlook or a negative one. You only have a bad day if you allow yourself to view it as such. I know that may sound overly simplistic, but the truth is that having a good attitude is very simplistic. We all go wrong when we let our internal critic convince us that we must have a certain set of circumstance to have a positive outlook. This is the critic who says, "I'll have a great attitude and positive outlook as soon as I:"

- ♦ Get a promotion.
- ♦ Make a million dollars.
- ♦ Find the right soul mate.
- ♦ Buy a bigger house, car, etc.
- ♦ Get out of debt.
- ♦ Lose weight.
- ♦ Get a college degree.

The sad thing is that none of these things will make you happy or give you a positive attitude about your life. Why? Because *things* don't bring happiness. These may all be goals for your life, but you can choose to be happy and positive now as you are reaching for those goals rather than bitter and despondent because you haven't reached them yet.

The key is to squelch the inner critic and convince yourself that you are worthy of the same respect as someone who has reached every goal on the list above. The fact that you're not quite there yet doesn't diminish you as a person in any way, and therefore it shouldn't affect your view of the world.

Many people take every setback or obstacle in life personally. As children we were taught to play to win, and if you don't win then there will be another game where you will have another chance to win. Somehow, as adults, we lose this perspective. It is easy to internalize every defeat and setback into a constant negative stream of dialogue that your internal critic is more than willing to use against you if you allow it. That dialogue might sound something like this:

4

- ◆ It's not my fault the boss likes him better than me.
- ◆ I'm not smart enough to figure out this project.
- ◆ If I ask for help I'll look incompetent.
- ◆ Why didn't I get my degree?
- ◆ Why can't I lose 20 pounds?
- ◆ Life just isn't fair - everyone gets breaks but me.

Thus life becomes a stream of "shoulda, woulda, coulda" regrets that interfere with your ability to move on and have the successful life you dream about. I know that may come as a surprise to some of you, that no one and no circumstance is holding you back except your own internal critic. Nevertheless, this is the case. A good example of this is a woman I know named Lacy. Lacy had three small children, a high school diploma, and no job experience when she and her husband divorced.

"I struggled through that first year working as a convenience store clerk in a small town and just trying to pay the bills. It took about thirteen months for me to finally reach the point were I had to make a decision. I could either live as I was and continue to struggle knowing I could never provide any hope for a future for my kids, or I could change my life."

Fortunately, Lacy chose to change her life. She sat down one evening and made a list of everything she wanted, and the first thing on that list was a college degree.

> *"I was surprised at the reaction of my family when I told them my plans to move me and my children one hundred miles away so I could attend college. I expected support, but I got a range of negative emotions – from the insinuation that I would fail if I attempted to get a degree, to dire warnings that my kids would grow up to be gang members because I was spending time in school. It hurt, but I'd already promised myself that I would make it work. I didn't have anything but a positive attitude and belief in myself, but it turns out that a positive attitude was all that I needed."*

Lacy struggled for several years working two jobs and going to school at night, but she did earn her degree. And then she earned another. Now with an MBA, Lacy recently witnessed her first child's graduation from college.

> *"I'm completely convinced that if I hadn't taken the risk of failing, I'd never have been able to succeed. While it was frightening at the time, now I look back on it as the best decision I ever made. Over the last twelve years, every time I was confronted with a big decision I thought about that day I drove away from everything that I had ever known. I know now that nothing can stand in my way, and I won't allow myself to ever feel defeated again."*

Lacy is a great example of the fact that you can either be controlled by attitude or you can choose to have your attitude under control. She chose to have her attitude under control and not be defeated by the negative comments and dire warnings, even from those closest to her.

Someone who has her attitude under control knows that there are things she absolutely can't change. Bad things can and do happen to people everyday. But people like Lacy have discovered that they can control how they respond to the bad things that happen. They choose to be optimistic and view problems as temporary issues. By doing this they are able to focus on solutions rather than being overwhelmed by the problems.

In contrast, someone who does not have his attitude under control generally lacks faith in himself and has no idea how much power he truly possesses. When bad things happen, such people tend to crumble under the weight of circumstance and become "victims" of external forces. For people who make this kind of thinking a habit, life is just a series of seemingly insurmountable difficulties. They become convinced that the powers-that-be-hate them, and they adopt a fatalistic attitude - an expectation of defeat that is a "self-fulfilling prophecy." They will allow their internal critic to tell them that it is no use working to have a better life since they will fail anyway, so why try? They believe these lies and cease trying to improve themselves. They soon find that their lives have become cycles of pessimistic drudgery, and they often feel and act doomed. And do you know what's really sad? The only payoff for them is this: They get to be right.

One of my favorite quotes is from the 1939 film *The Wizard of Oz*. When Glenda the Good Witch shows Dorothy that she can simply click her heels to return home, she tells a surprised Dorothy, "You had the power all along." This is true of most people today. They go through life searching for the illusive ideas of success and happiness only to find that it existed within them the whole time. Once you understand that happiness and success are yours to create, you are ready to build a successful attitude.

INSIDE OUT

In order to be truly happy, you must look inside yourself. The sad truth is that if you rely on happiness from external sources, let's say your job, your family, or your spouse, you will always be disappointed. Not because they intentionally mean to hurt you, but these sources rely on other people, and people are imperfect just as you are. If you focus on improving yourself and strive toward finding the joy within your own life, then all of your relationships with other people will improve. They will notice your new attitude, and they will see that you are no longer battered by circumstances as they are, and they will ask your secret. Now you might think it is impossible to have a great attitude if your life is in the toilet, but I heard a story recently that proves differently.

Michelle, an HR Director for a large legal firm, had a hard time keeping receptionists. The receptionists they hired had to deal with upset clients, demanding bosses, and frustrated co-workers. Very few stayed more than a few months. After a long progression of temporary employees, Michelle finally hired an older woman named Susan who had recently lost her husband.

"Susan hadn't worked in over twenty years, but I needed someone steady, and she needed the job. The law partners speculated that she wouldn't last the week, knowing how harsh this particular work environment could be. They told me I was crazy, and I almost believed them, wondering if she would even show up for work. Nevertheless, that first morning Susan arrived and took her place. As each employee came in, she greeted them with a smile and said, "Good morning, how are you?" Most of the employees and even the law partners were taken aback at her positive attitude. I have to admit I thought Susan only had a good attitude because she was so desperate for a job.

"But as the weeks wore on, Susan continued her morning greeting, and even our clients commented on how nice it was to talk to such an upbeat person every day. Over time, more and more employees soaked up that same positive attitude, and in less than a year the firm had turned into a great place to work. I'm still amazed that one person, in the lowest paid position in the company, can have that kind of power."

START TODAY

One of the wonderful things about being human is that we all have the ability to change ourselves. Many people have experienced the glory of a transformational epiphany that redirects their lives. They stepped back and recognized the kind of power that exists in each one of us, and then they set out to harness that power for themselves. That is what you are going to do. And it starts by reshaping your own ideas and thoughts – about *you*.

In order to do this, we have to understand where some of your negative attitudes and beliefs are coming from. This doesn't mean assessing blame. Understand that our brains are programmed throughout our lives and over time, by things we are taught, by experiences we have, and by people around us. Not all of the things that we learn or believe about ourselves are good, but these ideas form the basis of our internal dialogue.

Part of your internal dialogue may tell you that you aren't very smart, or that you aren't interested in the right things, or that the things you want are out of reach. There is an old saying that "misery loves company." Unfortunately, when one person in a particular peer group strives to achieve something beyond what those in the group perceive to be the norm, the reaction is often negative rather than positive. We all live in a certain comfort zone, and if one of the individuals within that zone steps up to a new level, the others will instinctively try to pull him back. This is an interesting reaction that is *not* unique to humans, but we humans seem to do it more and better than other animals. We are social creatures and want to belong to a group. But if that group is holding you back, then you must go forward even if it means losing some of those connections.

Our "group-think" mentality exists mostly out of fear. These are fears of various kinds: fear of failure, fear of success (it's true!) fear of the unknown, and even fear of loss. Though the people in your social or family circle may give you negative feedback, they will be convinced they are saving you from disaster. If we look back at the example of Lucy moving her children away to attend school, we recognize that her family didn't discourage her due to lack of love or emotion. They discouraged her due to their own fears. They wanted her to stay where it was "safe."

For many people this resistance to change sets up an attitude of helplessness, as in "I am damned if I do, and damned if I don't." Some will spend their entire lives in this limbo, yearning for a better life without the courage to pursue it. They often become bitter and frustrated, having nothing to show for their lives but wasted dreams. Realize now that time is short, and dreams are to be grasped, not heaped onto a pile of regrets.

"Change your thoughts and change your world."
~ Norman Vincent Peale ~

POSITIVE IDEAS

The first step to getting rid of an attitude of helplessness is to clear your mind of the negative dialogue from your internal critic. Negative thoughts build upon one another over time and crush your spirit. This could lead to bouts of depression and self pity.

10

I'm going to share a story with you from my buddy Chris in the United States:

> *"My freshman year in high school, our basketball team consisted of only thirteen players, and none of us were very good. We played teams that had a deeper line-up and much more talent. We had gotten trounced on a regular basis, and the season was half over. One day the coach sat the whole team down and gave us a long talk. He spoke about each of our positive attributes and about how he knew in his heart that we were winners. He said that from that day on, we would start every practice by closing our eyes and visualizing winning the state tournament."*

> *"I have to admit we were all pretty skeptical, but we were also tired of losing, so we did it. We closed our eyes for five minutes while Coach told us how we'd feel standing on the court receiving our trophy, cutting down the net, coming home to a hero's welcome. We won two games that season. Coach decided that we really hadn't bought into the idea that we could go all the way to the state championship playoffs. So he decided we needed to see it in person."*

> *"Some of the players and even some of the parents thought this was a foolish idea. Who did he think we were? The Harlem Globe Trotters? We were a small team from a tiny little town, and he had no business getting our hopes up.*

But coach persisted and finally convinced the school board to send us."

"We walked into the arena in awe. It was the kind of awe that makes you feel like a little speck of dust on the planet. We watched every game from beginning to end, talked to the players, and rooted for our favorite teams right along with the crowd. On the way home, we stayed up all night evaluating what we had seen and talking about what changes we had to make to get there."

"The next year we again started each practice visualizing victory, only this time we had been there. We'd seen it, tasted it, and felt it. We'd witnessed kids just like us living the dream we wanted, and now we were convinced we could do it. We practiced hard and played hard and won our district. Though we didn't get past regional play-offs, we had come much closer to going to state play-offs. The next year we stepped it up a notch, practicing harder and playing our hearts out. Again, we made it to regional play-offs and no farther."

"The trip home was depressing, and a couple of the players thought this was it. This is as good as we're ever going to be. Coach overheard the talk and immediately stopped the bus. He opened the door and asked all the players to get off the bus. We stood out by the road shivering in the cold as he told us that we'd come a long way and accomplished a lot. Then he said that he knew now why we hadn't gotten past regional play-offs. There were still a few among us that didn't believe we were good enough, and those people were stopping the rest of the team from getting to the state finals."

"He told us that each person had to make a decision. Either we would have the attitude of a team that was good enough to go to state, or we'd have an attitude of a team that would win state. He said that anyone that even thought about

*having a negative attitude didn't belong on his bus, because
it was a winner's bus. Needless to say, we all got back on
the bus, and not one more negative word was said. Sure
enough, the next year we experienced that awe once again
as we walked onto the court at the state tournament, this
time as players. We had won the right to be there, we had
worked hard, and we deserved it."*

This coach provided one of the clearest examples of the power of having a positive attitude. I suggest you take the same approach when dealing with your own negative thoughts. Stop the bus and get them off. They will only limit your forward progress.

DEMONS OF DESTRUCTIVE DIALOGUE

There are three basic categories of destructive dialogue. Chances are you fall into at least one of these categories. These demons are named Regret, Indecision, and Fear.

1. DEMON OF REGRET

The Demon of Regret gets everyone on occasion. His bag of tricks includes unfinished business, shattered relationships, and plans that went wrong. He haunts peoples' thoughts by making them hesitant and overly cautious. Some of his favorite negative dialogue includes the "what ifs."

WHAT IF:

♦ I had tried harder in that relationship?

♦ Not taken my spouse (or parents, etc.) for granted?

♦ I had let someone else drive?

♦ I had told my kids I loved them more?

♦ I hadn't given in and made a stupid mistake?

♦ I had keep my thoughts to myself?

♦ I had finished school?

This type of destructive dialogue only gets worse with time. If you don't learn to let go of the past, it will keep growing and growing until it overwhelms your present and destroys your future.

2. DEMON OF INDECISION

This demon is the present reality for many people. Even though daily life is a mix of good and bad, they respond with a negative attitude. Faced with more and more financial and family demands, they become paralyzed. Afraid of making the wrong decision, they make no decision at all and simply watch as life spins out of control. This demon's negative dialogue can sound like this:

♦ My boss has overloaded me with projects. Where do I turn?

♦ My spouse is unhappy. How can I help?

♦ I'm drowning in debt and can't make my payments. What can I do?

♦ I've just lost my job. What do I tell my family?

♦ I just graduated with loads of debt and no job. What now?

The main weapon you have for dealing with this demon is focus. Focus on the solutions. Take out a piece of paper and write down every possible option you can think of. Then ask family and friends to add options they know of. By allowing yourself to explore all the possibilities, you are moving forward. You will be able to find better and faster solutions by performing this exercise than if you just sat and worried about them. The key to dealing with the everyday stress of life is to force yourself forward, even if the Demon of Indecision tugs at you.

3. DEMON OF FEAR

This is a big one for most people. This demon's biggest weapon is the power of "if." This demon convinces people that the worst is just on the horizon, and they should watch out for falling pieces of sky and flying farm animals. His destructive dialogue usually focuses on the possible problems rather than the opportunities.

WHAT WILL I DO IF:

- ◆ I get fired?
- ◆ I get sick?
- ◆ I can't pay my bills?
- ◆ I can't ever find a spouse?
- ◆ My spouse divorces me?
- ◆ Terrorists invade our country?
- ◆ The stock market crashes?
- ◆ I lose everything?

I'll be the first to admit that planning for the future is a good thing. However, there is a difference between planning ahead and relentlessly obsessing. If you fixate on a problem, it is easy to become paralyzed. However, if you look to the future for solutions you are taking some portion of control over your life that will free you of this demon.

BEGIN AT THE BEGINNING

So what would cause you to have a habitual bad attitude? Why would you constantly live in fear, raining on other people's parades, not choosing to live an abundant and happy life? There are many possibilities, but most stem from past experiences and events in your own life. Let's look at a few possibilities.

INABILITY TO RELEASE PAST HURTS

If you have had a conflict with a family member or co-worker, it can give you an attitude of resentment and anger. Do you feel that anger resurface every time you see this person? Do you lie awake at night thinking about the conflict? Do you wish the person harm? If so, then you have not let go of the conflict. This causes an attitude that hurts you more than anyone else and can poison your current relationships.

LOW SELF ESTEEM

Do you avoid taking on new responsibilities so you won't risk failure? Do you put others down rather than congratulate their accomplishments? Do you refuse to assist co-workers for fear they may be after your job? If you find yourself with this kind of attitude, it may stem from low self esteem. You just don't believe in yourself or your abilities. Individuals with low self esteem usually try to protect what they have rather than believe they can have more. The problem is that this negative attitude actually has the opposite effect. By refusing to help others and move forward, you may become the least-needed member of the group.

FEAR

Fear is a natural emotion that protects us from danger. The problem is that many people imagine danger that does not exist or is minimal, and then they project that fear to be larger than life. This is paralyzing. A person living in fear will refuse to consider doing anything beyond his own idea of what is possible. People in the grip of fear would rather not try at all than have something bad happen, such as failing. These people also project their own fears onto those around them, encircling everyone they know with negative energy. They can't handle any type of change without feeling threatened or having an overall sense of impending doom.

STRESS

This is a big one. Everyone feels stressed on occasion, and no one is immune. The problem comes when that stress is allowed to build, day after day and week after week, until it affects every part of your daily life. Stress will make you short-tempered, give you stomach problems, interfere with your ability to sleep, and may even produce thoughts of suicide just to escape the relentless pressure. Stress can give you a very negative attitude for a few days, or for years. Alleviating the stress in your life takes effort. After all, it didn't build up overnight, and it probably won't go away overnight. But it's hard to create solutions if your mind is churning, and your first challenge is to stop thinking and start relaxing – both your mind and your body.

It is important to remember that you do have the power to change all of these problems in your life, but you must develop a plan. You have to sit down and first figure out what needs changing, and then write down possible solutions. Janet, an accountant and mother of two, tells how she did this in her life.

"When I first heard the idea that I could change my attitude and my life, I thought, 'Boy you don't have a clue about my life.' I felt like I was running at full speed for eighteen hours a day, and I was. Trying to get the kids to school, keep my work on track, and then go from soccer games to Cub Scouts was running me ragged. I got sick, couldn't eat, and had trouble sleeping. Finally, I couldn't take it anymore. My husband and I sat down and made a list of all the things we were doing. We talked about things we could cut out and how to share some other responsibilities and work together to handle the demands. It was very liberating. I had always thought that I was supposed to be able to do it all, have a career and a family, and that life would just magically be happy. I was afraid that if I asked for help or admitted that I couldn't do something I wasn't living up to everyone else's expectations, and that would mean I was a failure. My husband assumed that because I always insisted on doing everything myself I didn't trust him to do anything, so he never offered. By sharing our fears and concerns, the stress was lifted. Don't get me wrong; our lives were still basically the same, but how we handled the stress was completely different. My attitude went from getting up every morning with a sense of dread to looking forward to each day and enjoying my work and my family."

MONITORING YOUR ATTITUDE

One of the most important steps you can take in developing a new and successful attitude is to recognize when you are falling into a negative attitude. Maintaining self-awareness is a skill anyone can learn. By being conscious of the attitude you are projecting, you can ask yourself hard questions and determine where that attitude is coming from and how to change it.

For example, do you ever get angry in traffic? Who hasn't, right? But why? Is being angry going to get you there faster? No. Is the anger going to affect the rest of your morning or even the whole day? Probably. Practice letting that emotion go. Listen to great music, buy a book you love on CD and listen to it while you drive, but *release the anger.* Remind yourself that the negative energy doesn't affect the drivers in the other vehicles; it only hurts you. So let it go.

Once you get in the habit of examining your own attitude in daily situations you will also begin to notice others' attitudes. People naturally want to be with those who have a positive outlook. Notice how these positive people go through their day and how others respond to a good attitude. This is what you want to achieve.

"A great attitude does much more than turn on the lights in our worlds; it seems to magically connect us to all sorts of serendipitous opportunities that were somehow absent before the change."
~ Earl Nightingale ~

ATTITUDE TEST

Now you are ready to assess your own attitude and develop ways to deal with the stress in your life. We are going to go through a series of questions so you can determine which attitudes are holding you back.

1. HOW DO YOU RESPOND TO CONFLICT AT WORK?
   A. Avoid it

   B. Get angry

   C. Feel helpless

   D. Accept it as a challenge

2. HOW DO YOU VIEW YOUR SKILLS AND COMPETENCY?
   A. Less than my co-workers'

   B. Good enough

   C. Better than most

   D. Excellent

3. HOW DO YOU VIEW YOUR SOCIAL SKILLS
   A. Nonexistent

   B. Fair

   C. I'm at ease in social situations

   D. I can talk to anyone.

4. YOU FEEL GOOD ABOUT YOURSELF BASED ON WHAT OTHERS THINK

A. All the time

B. Most of the time

C. Sometimes

D. Rarely

5. YOU FEEL THAT IMAGINING A NEW AND SUCCESSFUL LIFE FOR YOURSELF IS

A. Unrealistic

B. Might be possible under the right circumstances

C. Will take more work than I'm willing to put in right now

D. Within my grasp and exciting to think about

If you scored mostly D's then you are ready to move forward and grasp the opportunities presented to you to make a better life.

If you scored mostly C's then you are right on the verge of making the kind of necessary changes to have the success you dream of. You will benefit a great deal from the following chapters to put you over the top in self-confidence and to develop a successful attitude.

If you scored mostly B's then you will need to seriously evaluate where your negative attitudes stem from and address those. The lack of self esteem and fear of the future may be holding you back or paralyzing your thoughts. I will show you how to unlock your potential for positive thinking and get past the bad experiences and events of your life.

19

THE MILLIONAIRE GENIUS

If you scored mostly A's then I would encourage you to seek professional counseling. Some issues from your past may have scared you too deeply to move beyond them on your own. This is okay. Every person goes through bad events, but some affect individuals more than others. Issues of abuse, addiction and co-dependent relationships must be dealt with on a professional basis. Then you will be ready to move toward a better life.

Most people who take this simple test get a mixed score. You may have some C's and a couple of B's, for example. This is not unusual. You will find that in some areas of your life, change will be easier to implement than in others. So you may progress at an uneven rate - which is fine, as long as you progress.

It may be easier for you to start with a good attitude at home while you try to change the issues you are dealing with at work. This may even include finding another job if you find that you are unable to progress where you are. It's up to you to decide. You can change jobs, cities, and family situations just by making the decision for what is best in your life and acting on it.

~ Notes ~

∽ *Notes* ∽

～ *Notes* ～

~ Notes ~

CHAPTER TWO

Super Beliefs

CHAPTER TWO

SUPER BELIEFS

Who do you believe yourself to be? It may seem a ridiculous question, but do you really know? And do you have the ability to change your own beliefs about yourself and your abilities? The answer is absolutely yes. If you watch any number of medical or psychological television programs that grace the small screen these days, many of these programs focus on the issues and questions surrounding the scientific debate known as "nature versus nurture." What the answer to this question means is, are we genetically destined to behave in certain ways, or can we consciously decide to behave differently by manipulating our environment? Researchers in the social sciences have spent a lot of time studying this question. Many of these studies involve families with adopted children; others study identical twins who were raised separately. The most important result of these studies shows that personal choices about one's lifestyle and environment can allow him to overcome a genetic predisposition to almost anything.

Still, many people have bought into the idea that their lives are predetermined, that they don't have much, if any, choice in how things turn out. They live with a fatalistic sense of the world, as in, "My family has never gone to college, so it's not meant for me to either" Or, "I've never lived anywhere else, so I can't move no matter how bad things are here." This is the "it's not my fault" attitude that is so common (and detrimental) in our world today. By not taking responsibility or control of their actions, these people continue to make poor choices that affect themselves and their children, etching a destructive behavioral cycle into society.

While this may be an oversimplification, we all can be guilty of having this attitude on occasion. We stop ourselves from dreaming too big, wanting too much, or living better than we think we should. Why? Who's to say what dream is too big or how much money is too much? Why do we actively choose to limit ourselves?

Jennifer is a graduating senior from Duke University, President of the Christian Intervarsity League, and a Mexican-American. She recalls coming face to face with her own ideas of limitations.

> *"My mother has always been big on education, so I always assumed I would go to college. My parents divorced when I was little, and when I got into high school I asked my dad what he thought about colleges. He told me that college was a waste for girls, and I needed to settle down and find a good man. I was devastated. Though I realize now that he spoke out of fear – since he'd never been to college and he didn't want to see me fail – it still hurt.*

> *"Even though I was determined to go anyway, the idea that I was expecting too much, and might ultimately fail, became lodged in my brain. When I got accepted into Duke I told my mom that I had decided to go to Texas Tech instead. It was only a couple of hours from home, and most of my friends were going there. She was shocked and upset that I chose to limit my options when one of the greatest opportunities of my life lay within my grasp. After much arguing she convinced me to spend at least one semester at Duke, and if I didn't like it I could come home.*

> *"Needless to say, I came to North Carolina and never looked back. I am so grateful that I didn't let Dad's words keep me from experiencing all the great things that I've been through at Duke these past four years."*

27

People develop their beliefs about what they can or can't accomplish from even the smallest incidents, like Jennifer experienced. Words spoken out of fear by a parent when she was just a teen could have limited her whole outlook on what she could accomplish and who she might become. Likewise, the same may be true of you. You may have family members or friends who constantly tell you to quit dreaming and focus on reality. You have to decide if you will let them limit your life. You have to decide if you will live in someone else's reality or create your own.

Each one of us must remember that it is not what we are born with or without that determines who we will become. And by the same token, you cannot blame others for your success or failure because this is the road to irresponsibility and helplessness. You can only change yourself and the way you relate to other people. This is the path to true happiness and success. Knowing that you are in complete and total control of your own destiny, no matter what happens or what others say, gives you the freedom to find your true self and determine who you will become.

Another destructive belief that many people hold onto is the "victim syndrome." This does not mean that you haven't experienced an unfortunate turn of events, but you must remember that it is not the event that determines the outcome. It is your reaction to that event. If you decide to face each difficulty with the attitude of "poor me," then that is exactly what you will get, a poor life. Viewing yourself as a victim of life rather than an active participant weakens your resolve, and it is very easy to feel trapped and remain the victim for your whole life.

MANY TIMES SOMEONE CAUGHT IN THE "POOR ME" CYCLE WILL SOUND SOMETHING LIKE THIS:

- My boss is always undermining me.
- I can't seem to catch a break.
- If there's a loser within 100 miles, I've dated him.
- My wife thinks I'm made of money.
- I can't help it if there just aren't any jobs right now.

The next time you catch yourself exhibiting "poor me" behavior, try relating your problems to people by starting every sentence with the word "I."

Once you begin to use this technique as an excuse for your behavior, you will discover immediately how negative and destructive playing the victim really is. You will also find that you are not really a victim, in most circumstances, except in your own mind. You have the power to change if you want to.

- I choose to stay in my job though I am frustrated and unhappy.
- I allow my family to pressure me financially because I am afraid to say no.
- I choose to date people that I know I won't like because I'm afraid of commitment.
- I like people to feel sorry for me because I have it so hard.

Another destructive behavior that may be limiting your belief in yourself is that of the "excuse maker." The excuse maker is incredibly creative when it comes to avoiding or putting off their goals. I know. I was one of these. And many times I sounded something like this:

- I'm too tired.
- I don't have enough time.
- I have too many other responsibilities.
- I'm too old.
- I'm too busy.

You name it and I made an excuse for it, until I realized that I had excused myself right out of living. Alcoholics Anonymous has a saying, "There are a million excuses for picking up a drink, but no good reason." And it's true. Have you excused yourself from a college education? From

THE MILLIONAIRE GENIUS

making more money? From finding a great relationship? Excuses abound, but real reasons are few. Take responsibility for yourself and stop making excuses.

I'M IN CHARGE

30

So how do you begin to change your beliefs about yourself? The first thing to do is to stop lying to yourself. We all do it, but that doesn't help us – it just means we have lots of company. How many times have you promised yourself not to spend too much, then you went out and get a new pair of shoes or something "for the kids?" John is a good example of a reformed self-fibber.

"My wife, Sherry, and I made a pact that we would each lose twenty pounds last summer before our anniversary cruise. The first week or so I did really well. Then I found myself sneaking by the donut shop, or running by the store to pick up snacks, all the time justifying my behavior by saying it was 'for the kids.' Sherry, meanwhile, stuck to the plan.

"As the date of the cruise approached, I became more and more short-tempered and disgusted with myself because I was disappointed that I hadn't lost even five pounds while Sherry had already met her goal. I didn't realize how my behavior was affecting everyone in the family until one night she came to me and said she thought the cruise was a bad idea.

"I couldn't believe it. We'd planned this for almost a year, and I had let my self-deception almost ruin it. I immediately apologized, and we did go on the cruise, but it was a good lesson for me that people who lie to themselves end up angry and disgusted with their behavior, and it shows."

SELF PERCEPTION

Have you ever gone to the carnival funhouse and looked at yourself in the mirrors? If you have then you are aware of how distorted and silly those images are. Yet many people walk around with just as distorted an image of themselves in their minds every day. They tell themselves, "I'm a loser." "I don't deserve this." "I'm stupid."

Why does this happen? Why do we let ourselves believe the worst and then perceive that to be reality? The human mind is a fabulous tool. It has amazing coping skills to allow us to exist and survive under intense and adverse circumstances. A good example of this is what happens to prisoners of war.

If held in captivity long enough, prisoners begin to perceive their world in the context of prison life only, and thoughts of escape or going back to a regular life fade far into the back of their minds. They cope with daily life, torture, and constant abuse by becoming immune to the horror of it. Eventually it becomes their new reality, and they don't consciously think of it anymore.

This is also true to a much lesser extent in our own daily lives. If you work for a verbally abusive boss, over time the abuse seems almost normal, and your mind allows you to cope with it so you can exist in the situation. However, the effect on your sense of well being is devastated while you weren't aware it was happening. Though external sources may affect your ideas of who you are, the worst and toughest source is yourself.

If you constantly allow your internal critic to tell you that you aren't good enough, smart enough, or "whatever" enough, then eventually you will buy into that thought process and believe it. You will have fulfilled your own negative predictions and will be viewing the world as a distorted image through a set of negative filters.

31

THE MILLIONAIRE GENIUS

All of us are capable of distorting the truth or missing it entirely, especially when we are dealing with a stressful situation. Just read the interviews from a group of people in the same traffic accident. They will run the gamut from horrible to no big deal. Everyone perceives and remembers things differently in each situation. The perception or memory you have may not be the truth, but if you believe and buy into it, your future reality will be affected. A company near my home recently announced that it would scale back raises to only one percent due to bad sales figures for the year. Two of my good friends work for this company, and I agreed to meet them for lunch.

Carl arrived a few minutes early with his head hanging, claiming he didn't have much of an appetite. "Can you believe them? The company president makes over two million a year; I'll bet he doesn't get a lousy one- percent raise," Carl complained. "And I know exactly why we aren't making money. All those sales people ever do is take clients out to dinner and drink, while we working stiffs pay for it." He continued his rant for a few more minutes until Matt joined us.

"Sorry, had to call my wife. I was too excited to wait." He had a huge smile on his face. "I just knew they were going to announce layoffs, and not only did they not lay anybody off, they're giving us a raise! You can't beat that."

I sat there dumbfounded for a minute trying to figure out if these guys had been at the same meeting. Obviously they had, but their perceptions of what they heard were at opposite ends of the spectrum. Carl filtered what he heard through his perception and expectation that he deserved much better. Matt filtered what he heard through a grateful heart and positive attitude. Each man chose how he reacted to the news; one was positive and upbeat, the other was negative and angry.

The problem with allowing our perceptions to go unchecked is that they soon become reality, just like the prisoner of war. There is an old saying that a lie unchallenged soon becomes the truth. And our minds will make it so. Have you allowed your perceptions to be altered so that the life you are living has become a distortion of reality? Have you become so caught up in the struggle of everyday life with bills, kids, marriage, and work that you don't even recognize that there are opportunities all around you?

LIMITING PERCEPTIONS

One of the biggest problems with distorted perceptions is that they become, by definition, limiting. How many times have you run into people who had an unshakable faith that they would persevere? One example of this might be Donald Trump. Here's a billionaire real estate mogul who has lost everything even to the point of bankruptcy, endured two messy divorces, and has been made fun of on late night television; yet he has risen from the ashes to regain his millions, marry a beautiful woman, and score his own reality television show. He has an unshakable faith in his own ability to succeed, and it shows. But few people you meet are like this.

Most people's perceptions of themselves include a long list of "can't do's." We spend our time convincing ourselves that we aren't good enough, while people like Donald Trump spend their time convincing themselves that they are the best.

So how do we stop this madness? First you must be aware. Just as you become aware of your own bad attitudes, you must also become aware of the lies you tell yourself everyday. You may have the best of intentions, but the self-perceptions that have been ingrained since childhood can be very difficult to get rid of. You may float along, working on your attitude, trying to perceive everything in a positive light, when BAM! A stressful situation presents itself, and you react with the same old negative emotions. Rather than feeling defeated, there are three tools you can use to help get your mind back on track to a positive outlook.

1. THIS IS NOT GOING TO LAST FOREVER.

While it may seem like it at the time, no trial or tribulation lasts forever. I've never figured out why it is that when something good happens it's forgotten very quickly, yet when something bad happens it seems like it attaches itself to our brains and gets dragged around for all eternity. It does take time to get past some problems, but there is a process. It's part of who we are as humans. Give yourself over to the recovery process and get on with things. When you look back, you want to see this trial as something you endured and triumphed over, rather than a black spot of self pity in your past.

2. THIS WILL NOT DESTROY MY ENTIRE LIFE.

What do you think Martha Stewart thought when they slapped the cuffs on her wrists and dragged her off to jail? "This is it?" "My life is over?" She easily could have thought that, and she probably had moments when she did. But then she picked herself up and started again, and you can, too. No matter what the situation, losing a job, getting divorced, or the death of a loved one, the emotions you are feeling will fade over time, and you will go on with your life. There may be changes that you must deal with, but you will get through it.

3. THIS KIND OF STUFF HAPPENS TO EVERYONE.

Life is a stream of random events that affect everyone at some point. You haven't been singled out or made to suffer any more or less because of who you are or aren't. You can't take these events personally or internalize the negative emotions as something you deserve. This will only serve to bring more negative thoughts and emotions your way and compound your problems. Search for solutions, do the best you can, and move on after having learned valuable coping skills that will help you get through the next event life throws your way.

As we have already talked about, the power of another person's words on you can be extreme. As you might already have guessed, the same is true of you. Each day, you are shaping the self perception and awareness of those around you, either in a positive or negative way. How your spouse and children react to you, as well as how your co-workers deal with you, will give you the clues you need to decide if you have a positive or negative influence on them. You should always be aware of what you say, particularly when under stress. Words can't be taken back. This brings up a very important tool that will allow you to mend relationships and accept yourself. That is forgiveness.

I know this is a simple, basic concept. But one of the best ways to rid yourself of a negative attitude is with forgiveness. This doesn't just mean forgiving those who have hurt you, which it does, but it also includes forgiving yourself.

Stop beating yourself up for past mistakes. If you were addicted to drugs or alcohol, odds are good that you hurt a lot of people. But you also hurt yourself. You have to forgive yourself to be able to move on and ask forgiveness of others.

Have you ever failed at a business venture or even declared bankruptcy like Donald Trump? Forgive yourself. Learn the harsh lessons, and do better next time. Have you just given up on another diet and thrown your hands up in frustration at your lack of will power? Forgive yourself and begin again. Have you just lit up a cigarette when you haven't smoked in months? Forgive yourself. Like the concepts of a positive attitude and the correct perception, forgiveness begins with you.

Some people find it hard to forgive themselves because they hold themselves to an unrealistically high standard. They are perfectionists. But even they can change, and so can you. If you accept that we are all human and will all make mistakes, then it becomes very natural to allow yourself to forgive. Once you have forgiven yourself, you are ready to address how your negative behavior has affected others.

Here are a few helpful hints to remember when seeking out the power of forgiveness:

- ◆ Time never runs out. No matter how many years it has been, you can always forgive and be forgiven. Even if that person is no longer living, you can still ask their forgiveness in your heart, then forgive yourself and move on.

- ◆ Not everyone will be thrilled. Some people who have known the old negative you, will be suspicious of your transformation and your request for forgiveness. That's fine. Do it anyway. You cannot control how people react to you; you can only control yourself. If they choose not to forgive, then you must be understanding and let it go.

- ◆ Don't fall into the trap of hiding painful memories or ignoring old hurts. You unconsciously carry around old grudges and emotions that weigh on you every day. They contribute to your negative internal dialogue without your even realizing it. Uncover those areas and events of your life and deal with them.

Several years ago a man in his sixties told me the story of the type of father he had been. Steve had been very harsh with his kids, correcting them for the smallest infraction and punishing them sometimes to the point of borderline abuse.

"I really didn't know any different at the time. My own father had been an alcoholic and a harsh disciplinarian. I thought that a good father made his children afraid of him and kept them in line with a belt and regular verbal tirades.

"Years later, after one of my children had been through several years of therapy, she wrote me a letter saying that she forgave me. At first I was offended; I thought I'd been a good father, and all my kids turned out to be fine people. It never occurred to me that I'd done them any harm at all.

"After months of thinking and praying about it, I realized that I needed to go to each of my children and ask for their forgiveness. It startled me that my two other children hadn't considered themselves adversely affected at all, while the one who wrote the letter was upset and angry. I realized she hadn't forgiven me at all, but had just sent the letter as an exercise designed by the therapist.

"I could have gotten angry and had a bad attitude about it, I suppose, but she really did me a favor. She allowed me to forgive my own father and let go of a lot of resentment that I'd had pent up all these years."

MOVING AHEAD

Once you have let go of the past and have emptied yourself of your negative emotions, you are ready to move forward. You are ready to seek out knowledge and understanding of how people behave, and how to use that to improve your life. You are also free to develop new beliefs about yourself and your life.

"That sounds great," you may be thinking, "but what's to prevent the old negative emotions from showing up again when things get tough?"

There is series of steps that you will need to master that will pull you through tough times and keep you on track for a successful life. We'll call this your "crisis kit." We'll start by using a real life example of how this works:

Clayton worked for eight years for a banking company. The company was bought out by a large firm, and many changes took place.

"Everyone had concerns that the new bosses would be eliminating positions as the companies were integrated, but I refused to dwell on it or let the fear get the best of me.

I continued to work hard and encourage those around me to do the same. A few weeks later I received notice that in ninety days my job would be absorbed into their existing structure, and I would be out of work. I remember driving home that day in a daze. 'How could this be happening? What would I do? How would my family survive?'

"*I called my brother and best friend and poured out all the concerns I had. They were supportive and helped me see that it wasn't the end of the world. They urged me to look at it as a positive thing. Now I would have the opportunity to advance my career in a new and different way.*

"*After a long night of worry, I realized that they were right. I stopped telling myself that this was a disaster and decided to come up with a plan to move my career forward. I also wrote down all the things that I needed to take care of in case I didn't find a job immediately.*

"*Once I had a plan, I got together with my co-workers and some of our past clients and got a feel for the job prospects. Several recommended options and made suggestions that proved invaluable. Meanwhile, I continued to work hard at my job, refusing to give in to the temptation of having a short-timer's attitude and not caring.*

"*One of our long-time clients who knew the situation commented on how dedicated I seemed to be and asked if I'd be interested in interviewing for a new project management position that they had open. Though I'd have never thought myself qualified, at his suggestion I applied for the job. I've been working for them now for over a year and love my new responsibilities. But it would have never happened if I'd let myself feel down and defeated by the circumstances.*"

CRISIS KIT

By using this tool kit, you will be able to release the worry and stress swirling around you when another crisis arises. There will still be very difficult times that you must weather, and there will be occasions when it seems like all is lost. But please remember that every setback is temporary as long as you force yourself to move forward.

* When faced with a crisis, use your fear as a motivating factor and take action. While you may spend a short time trying to deal with something unexpected, don't let yourself become paralyzed.

* Support others who may be experiencing the same crisis. This may include co-workers, family, and friends. Encourage them to not dwell on the worst but to consider all the options available to them. This will not only help people you care about, it will also help you by redirecting the focus of your thoughts from yourself to those around you.

* Talk about it. Sometimes the best thing you can do is share your concerns with others. This allows you to get your feelings out and then to deal with them. Sometimes just hearing yourself voice your problems makes them seem less scary.

* Monitor your inner critic. Bad things happen. It's part of everyday life. Don't fall into the trap of taking the crisis as a personal commentary on what kind of person you are.

* Plan ahead. Make a list of all the issues you will need to deal with during and after this crisis. Search out solutions before these issues become crises in their own right. Develop a plan that will help you cope down the road.

* Ask for help. Seek out individuals whose opinions you trust and ask their advice. Many times they will be able to see the situation much clearer than you can at the moment. Some individuals you know may have gone through a similar situation and will be able to lead you in the right direction and also point out pitfalls along the way.

♦ Maintain a positive routine. How you respond to the crisis will be noticed by those around you. If you allow yourself to respond poorly, you may miss opportunities that you would have had if your response had been positive and upbeat.

40 ◆ YOUR ONE MOTIVATING DESIRE

In order to have a successful life you need to determine what the single most motivating factor in your life is. This is the one thing that you will move heaven and earth to achieve.

It may be a single mom's wish to provide a great life for her kids. It may be a young man's dream to never have to worry about money again. It may be your dream of proving yourself in business. What is the single most motivating factor in your life?

Notice that I said "factor," I did not say goal. Though they may look very similar, goals are very specific steps on the path of success. Goals are concrete and defined, so there is no question when you reach them. Motivating factors are warm and fuzzy. They are the feelings you associate with success. They are the emotions that carry you through the tough times. They are the beliefs and desires you have for your future.

Think about the famous Charles Dickens' novel *A Christmas Carol*. This is one of my favorite novels because the motivations of the characters are very clear. One thing I find interesting is the character Bob Cratchet, the jovial father of a crippled son. Day after day he goes to work with a smile on his face and a spring in his step, even though the man he works for is too stingy to give him sufficient coal in his office fireplace to keep warm. So why does Tiny Tim's father work for a man as odious as Ebenezer Scrooge? Cratchet loves his family, and in order to provide for them he will do anything, including work for Scrooge. How many of you have worked for a boss who was almost as oppressive and difficult as Scrooge? Why?

The idea of a single motivating factor is a basic human trait. Most of us already have it deep inside of ourselves; we just need to expose that desire and then take steps to help us accomplish it. These steps are our goals. Once you define what your single motivating factor is, then you need to be able to motivate yourself on a daily basis. Some techniques you may use for self motivation include the following:

1. Positive Physical Appearance: You know how you feel when you look like a million bucks. Even if you are having a down day, by merely dressing up more than normal you already feel better about yourself. If you add to that a good posture and a smile you will convince everyone, including yourself, that things are moving in a positive direction.

2. Positive Memories: Sometimes just remembering positive events and interactions will help keep you motivated and moving toward your goals. Looking back on how far you've come and what you have accomplished will spur you on to bigger and better things.

3. Positive People: Spending time around other positive, upbeat people will improve your whole outlook. Make it a point to regularly spend time with people who are positive and are willing to laugh. Laughter has a soothing and healing effect on each person's heart. I know if I spend just a few minutes laughing with a friend or co-worker, the stress and trials of the day seem much lighter, and I am more willing to tackle the challenges.

4. Believe in yourself: Write down the positive actions and attributes you have exhibited on a weekly basis. Not only does this motivate you to keep the positive juices flowing for the next week, it can also be used as a stop-gap measure to identify if you have slipped back into a negative frame of mind. By reinforcing positive images and focusing on your good qualities you can build a well of resilience within yourself, allowing you to perform under even more stress. Acknowledging your

41

THE MILLIONAIRE GENIUS

strengths convinces you that you have strength to spare, and you do. The single most limiting thing that anyone ever does is to tell him/herself, "I can't."

5. Exercise and Sleep: Take care of yourself. It is very difficult to stay positive and motivated if you are tired and dragging. This may require some schedule rearranging and shuffling, but if it does then do it. People today lead jam-packed lives, allowing every minute of every day to be stolen away. This leaves no time for you. You are your own most valuable asset, so it is not in your best interest to allow yourself to become run down or sick. Don't be afraid to say "no" to one more meeting, one more volunteer event, or one more family function. Take some time for you.

> *"Desire is the key to motivation, but it's determination and commitment to an unrelenting pursuit of your goal – a commitment to excellence – that will enable you to attain the success you seek."*
>
> ~ Mario Andretti ~

∾ *Notes* ∾

~ *Notes* ~

~ Notes ~

~ *Notes* ~

CHAPTER THREE

Super Paradigm Shift

CHAPTER THREE

SUPER PARADIGM SHIFT

48

A paradigm is a pattern of thought which represents the beliefs of a person or group of people. The first two chapters of this book were designed to help you uncover the specific negative attitudes or beliefs that you have about yourself and your ability to succeed. Now that you have identified some or all of those beliefs, it is time to replace them with new, positive thoughts, feelings and actions. These will define the person you are to become and give you a road map that will allow you to earn more money, achieve greater success, and have a more satisfied life than you ever thought possible.

What we are doing is creating a "paradigm shift." We are shifting your negative attitudes and beliefs into positive ones, and as you change, those around you will respond to that change, and their own attitudes and beliefs will be affected for the better.

WHO DO YOU WANT TO BE?

It may seem a little strange to stop and consciously think about the kind of person you want to be, but if you are serious about changing your life you have to decide who you want to become.

The qualities that define truly happy, successful people are very different than those we see in the media everyday. You can turn on your television at any given moment and see the lifestyle of what I like to call a "Person with Money" (PWM).

The PWM might be a big-screen celebrity, a rock star, or even a business person who has become a celebrity in his/her own right. This individual tends to be very self-absorbed, self-important and self-indulgent. He/she only buys the best of everything, and that usually means the most expensive. They are seen with the "right" people, but usually for the wrong reasons. Their relationships and family lives are strained or nonexistent. Their children are overindulged and many times end up in rehab for one substance abuse or another. A PWM may garner our fascination and much media attention, but there are few who actually enjoy living their lives. Truth be told, many PWM's are miserable.

49

So how do you become successful and not end up just another PWM? By becoming a "Person of Quality" (POQ). This means immediately defining the qualities that you want to emulate. Being a POQ does not just happen. It takes planning and effort. Below are some of the characteristics that distinguish a "Person with Money" from a "Person of Quality:"

5 Traits of a Person of Quality

1. He or she has a strong desire to succeed mixed with personal humility. A POQ doesn't toot his own horn relentlessly. He determines a path and pursues it. Those around him see the progress of his efforts and note them without his ever having to say a word.

2. He or she acts with calm, quiet determination and adheres to high personal standards. POQ's tend not to be charismatic. They don't really draw crowds. They work with calm, quiet determination and honesty toward what they want.

3. POQ's frequently sit back and reflect on events, never blaming others or outside conditions for poor results. A POQ evaluates both positive and negative outcomes and ponders how he or she can improve. He or she doesn't blame circumstances or other individuals for his or her problems; a POQ meets them head on and deals with them in the most positive way possible.

THE MILLIONAIRE GENIUS

4. A POQ isn't afraid to give credit to others and rarely allows people to focus on him. A POQ will often credit all those around him for their help on his journey of success. As a result, more and more individuals who are impressed by his work ethic will join in to help as well. They know they will be recognized for their efforts and have no fear that they will be blamed for a bad result. This gives those around a POQ the freedom to give 100%.

5. They work with diligence and are not swayed by the "next big thing." A POQ adheres to her plan and works toward her goal with consistent diligence. POQ's are not swayed by a new money-making scheme, diet, or potential "opportunity of a lifetime." They quietly work toward their goals day after day.

Becoming a person of quality sounds easy, but it is not. It requires careful thought, planning, and constant evaluation.

Sahaad is a programmer in the tech industry. He tells of trying to implement his own POQ plan:

> *"Ever since I was small, I had a bad temper. I would become easily frustrated and lash out verbally at those around me. I spent years blaming my job, my wife, and my parents for my lack of success. My frustration grew worse and worse. My wife left me, and my co-workers avoided me. I slowly sank into a deep depression. I realized I had to make a change, and the only thing I had left to change was me. The idea of becoming a Person of Quality seemed like a shot in the dark, but I didn't have anything else, so I tried it."*

> *"The first people to notice were my co-workers. As I began to consciously give credit to others for their work, they offered suggestions and assistance with my projects. These were projects I had worked on for months with only a moderate amount of success, and they suddenly accelerated forward with the suggestions and input from my co-workers. While*

it was too late for my marriage, I resolved that my next
relationship would be different. And it has been. Not that
there aren't difficulties and problems from time to time,
there are. But now I can step back and rely on my plan
to always be a POQ. The frustrations and problems are
easier to deal with, and those around me are now eager to
help. My whole life has changed, but the only thing I really
changed was me."

So how do you put your POQ plan into action? By following a simple four step process. This includes:

1. Confronting Reality

2. Removing the Negative

3. Focusing on Your Plan

4. Having a Disciplined Lifestyle

STEP 1: CONFRONTING REALITY

We touched on this subject briefly in the first two chapters. In those sections we were looking inward, evaluating what makes you act the way you do. As you try to implement the POQ principles you will be confronted everyday with your former reality. This includes those who are skeptical of change, those who can't understand your need for change, and even those who hasten to point out every misstep and setback that you have along the road. Unfortunately, many times the people engaging in this behavior are the ones closest to you. Your friends and family, spouse and children, can make change very difficult. Those who you expect to support you maybe the very ones that put obstacles in your path.

I tell you this only by way of warning. You have to be prepared and think about how you will handle these situations in advance. This will allow you to adhere to your POQ principles and not overreact. If your spouse or parents constantly point out flaws or make fun of your plan, you have to be able to respond to their criticism in a positive way and still move forward. One way to do this is to allow them to have their say, then ask for their help. If you allow them to help you toward your dream, then they have invested ownership in that dream as well. While they may be your worst critics at first, as they see your success and hear you credit them for helping, they will often become your biggest supporters, fans and cheerleaders.

For each area of your life you must confront the reality that exists in order to deal with it. This includes your work, your personal relationships, and your lifestyle. In each of these areas you must conduct a similar survey and gather all the facts. Let's take your job as an example. You must make a sort of worksheet that includes the following:

1. Decide why you are here and how you got here. Do you want to change this aspect of your life? If so, why?

2. Speak with those around you and get their input with respect to either changing your job or staying where you are.

3. Review previous changes you have tried to make in this area. Why did or didn't they work? Could you have done anything differently? Have you accumulated knowledge that will help you move forward?

4. What are the catalysts or determining factors for change in this area?

These worksheets will be very important in determining what your life goals should be. It may seem like a lot of work to write all this down, but there is something about seeing your problem written out on paper that gives you a little bit of distance. It's like having an example in a math textbook. You see the problem for what it really is, and the solutions appear obvious. But in real life, when you don't consciously think through your actions and objectives things just seem to happen. This often leads you to a terrible place.

For another example of this kind of worksheet let's use Jane, a thirty-two year old Customer Service Representative in a call center.

JANE'S JOB REALITY WORKSHEET

1. How did I get here? *A friend worked here and suggested I apply. It was more money and had better benefits.* **Do I want to change this part of my life?** *Yes, I've gone as far as I can go and there is no more opportunity for advancement.*

2. What are the pros and cons for changing jobs?

PROS	CONS
Possibly have more money and opportunity for advancement	*Have seniority and good benefits*
Will have chance for more satisfying job off the phones	*Am knowledgeable and comfortable where I am*
Could have a new and better work environment and make new contacts	*Like the environment and all the contacts I have in my current job*
Could get a job closer to home with less travel time	*May have to commute longer distance*

3. What previous changes have I tried to make in this area and how have they turned out? *I had a series of jobs before this one; they were all in the service sector. I think I now have the experience to move on to something in the supervisory area and possibly finish my degree. My self-confidence is better, and I know I will get a good recommendation from my current employer.*

4. What is the catalyst for change? *What is stopping me? Fear and uncertainty that I might not be able to find another job and be stuck doing this forever. I also have been afraid that not having a degree will keep me from moving upward.*

Your worksheet may be similar, or it may be different from Jane's, but it still should contain all four areas to be useful. As you fill out the worksheets for each area of your life, it will become clear which outside influences are negative and which are positive. It will also become evident what you can change (job, location, etc.) and what you can't (family, friends, and co-workers). You can have a positive influence on the people around you, but you cannot change them.

This exercise sets you up for the next step in our plan: to remove or mitigate the negative items in your life.

Removing the Negative

This is one of the toughest areas you will have to confront. The reason is that it usually involves people, including those you care deeply about. You can get away from a negative work environment by changing jobs. You can get away from negative friends and acquaintances by relocating to a different area or city. But you can't get away from family and those you love. The relationships you have had and want to keep are the ones that you will have to confront and work on. You can't escape them, and you can't let things go.

This doesn't mean having a screaming argument with every member of your family. But it does mean that you should sit down and evaluate your relationship with every family member or friend and decide who is an overall positive or negative influence. Do certain members of your immediate family make you feel like you aren't good enough, or that you will fail at everything you try? Do they constantly disparage you to others? Do they ever have anything good to say to you or about you?

On the other hand, are there family members who are constantly supportive and uplifting? Do they offer ideas and suggestions? Do you find yourself at ease and able to laugh in their company?

Create a form for each person and think back over the relationship. Though you can't change other people, you will know who the positive influences are after this exercise. While I don't recommend abandoning your family, I would suggest that, at least on a temporary basis, you spend a little less time with those who are consistently negative and practice positive reactions to their negative comments and behaviors. On the other hand, spend a little more time with those in your life who are positive and soak up the good feelings and emotions. Those will carry you through many setbacks as you put your plan into motion.

Sometimes negative people, especially those in your family, will respond to a sincere and direct request from you to either refrain from showering you with negative comments or to balance the negative with some positive comments. If you believe it is worth it to make such a request by all means try it. At least you will be on record with them, and they may not have ever realized either what they were doing or how it was affecting you.

Over time, as you become more confident, you will be able to spend time around negative people and not let their attitudes affect you. You may also slowly change some of their own attitudes and beliefs, but even if you don't, you will have changed, and that is what is important.

Focusing on Your Plan

In the next chapter we will focus on goals and goal-setting; but before we do, you need to know what goals to set and what to expect from them. Remember that we talked in the first chapters about how important it is for you to forgive yourself for past mistakes? No matter what your goals or objectives are, there will be setbacks and missteps.

It is very easy to give up on your plan after one of these missteps and go back to life as you have previously known it. Change is hard, and it is easy to become downhearted and want to take the easiest path. You must decide right now, even before you truly know what your goals are, that you will stick to the steps. You must imagine failure and figure out how you will deal with it BEFORE it happens. This gives you a clear path that you have already practiced in your mind to avoid being dragged into despair or depression.

Instead of dwelling on past failures or negative events, imagine yourself taking charge and overcoming the obstacles you face. Let's use the job example again.

Have you ever thought about losing your job? Being laid off or even fired? Most people have thought about it, and some live in absolute fear that it will happen to them. But have you ever thought beyond that? What's next? If you lose your job today, what happens tomorrow? Do you lie in bed and wait for impending doom to set in? Not if you are a POQ. While it's hard to feel like a Person of Quality the day after being canned, you know that that's who you are. You get up and start a list of what you will do to have the most positive outcome possible. Your list might include all of your education and skills acquired at your last job. It may include a list of contacts who might know of an opening in a similar field or even a different field that might suit you.

The best way to focus on any plan is by action. By actively moving toward a goal you feel in control, and the worst thing about losing your job is that you feel out of control. Where will the money come from? What happens if I don't get something soon? Will I lose my house, car and everything I've worked for?

If you allow those negative thoughts to circulate in your head as you lie in bed staring at the ceiling, of course the worst will happen. But if you act immediately and start to work on improving your situation, then you will feel in control once again and will be able to do something about your situation instead of feeling helpless.

Once you have imagined the negative scenarios and events that may happen to you and you have formulated a plan to overcome them you still aren't ready to set goals, but you are ready to answer the next questions. And that is:

"WHAT IN THE WORLD DO I WANT TO DO WITH MY LIFE?"

This is a basic question, one that you probably asked yourself sometime around high school graduation, or maybe even college graduation. Now you are facing that question once again. What do you want your life to be? It may or may not have anything to do with the job you hold currently.

We all had dreams at some point, but for most of us life tends to get in the way. It may seem unrealistic to return to those dreams now, but it's not. If you are working at a job or continuing a relationship because you feel stuck in that mould, you are lying to yourself. You continue because that is easier than making a change. Now if you are already convinced that change is the road you wish to travel, then you must ask yourself the three following questions:

1. **What am I passionate about?** By passionate, I mean what kind of work or pursuit would you almost do for free? (NOTE: I said "almost.") What holds your interest for hours on end, and how do you spend the "free" time you have now?

2. **What can you be the best at?** What area of those things that you are passionate about can you excel in?

3. **What can you make money at?** After all, the ability to earn an income is a key factor in deciding what goals to set. You can participate in very fulfilling volunteer work your entire life and enjoy it immensely, but you still have to do something to pay the bills.

When you think about what occupation you want to pursue, you want to look for things that contain all three of these items. Not one, or two, BUT ALL THREE. You can be passionate and very good at what you do and still starve to death. You can make lots of money and also be good at your job, but still find yourself bored and unfulfilled. You can also find a job that you arc passionate about and that also makes a great deal of money, but if you can't excel at it you will soon find yourself in the unemployment line.

You may have several ideas right now. That's good. You may want to try them all. That's not so good. If you try a job (or relationship or whatever), then switch, then switch again, you lose the forward momentum and everything you have learned, and then you have to start all over from square one. When you are deciding which direction you want to head, you must focus all of your actions to build upon the prior action to achieve the greatest reward.

Let's take an example. Let's say that right now you are a low-to-midlevel sales manager. You have decided upon the following:

1. You want to go back to school.
2. You want to invest in real estate and have read numerous books on the subject.
3. You want to earn a six figure income.
4. You want to be your own boss.

What do you do? Let's take the obvious. You are already a sales manager, so you have sales skills. You have a passion and interest in investing, specifically in real estate. You want to earn a six figure income that you cannot earn at your present job, and you want to go back to school.

By combining all these goals, I'd project that your best opportunity may lie in getting your real estate license. You can go back to school for a very short period of time, then learn from other realtors how to invest in real estate profitably, and then perhaps even become a real estate broker and have your own business. This accomplishes every goal we listed and combines them in such a way to achieve the greatest return. Funneling all your activities toward a common goal will have a cumulative effect that is much more powerful than working at four separate goals.

HAVING A DISCIPLINED LIFESTYLE

I think everyone views discipline with apprehension. Discipline is synonymous with hard work, which is what this is. But discipline not only involves the work you do, it also pertains to the life you lead. Many times what you do isn't nearly as important as what you don't do.

We already talked about that fact that one of the biggest complaints people have today is stress. Yet most of their stress is self-inflicted. They make bad choices, overload their schedules, and do what is the easiest instead of the best.

The first aspect of a new, disciplined you, is the ability to say no. It is okay to say no to your friends, your family, your spouse, your children, to anyone. Not saying no just tells others that your time isn't worth anything. You are always available, no matter what hardship is placed on your family or your long-term goals. You have to stop the "cycle of worthlessness" by saying no.

The first step, as with the other areas we've talked about, is to sit down and make a list. List all the clubs, civic, and church groups that you are involved in. List all the work you do after hours or on weekends for your job. List all the classes, meetings, and shopping trips you make with friends. List lunches and dinners out, shopping trips, movie attendance, and other forms of entertainment.

Now look at your list. You must go through this list and cut these events down. Most people can cut their schedules by at least fifty percent, and you may be able to cut more. Do you have to go shopping every weekend, or can you make one or two trips a month? Do you have to have lunch out every day, or can you make it three times a week? Are you on four church committees instead of one or two?

You don't want to cut back? Then you don't want a new life. If you do what you have always done, you will get the same results you always have. Your time is your future. If you don't carve out some time for you and your plan, you will end up in this same spot next year, and the year after that. I'm not saying don't be involved, just use moderation.

Perhaps in order to go back to school you have to have at least two free nights per week. Be honest but firm with the people that you normally meet with on these nights. Most of the time they will understand and be supportive. Don't assume that someone will think less of you because you are unavailable. Have you tried being unavailable? You might be surprised that they go on just fine without you, leaving you the necessary time to work on yourself and your own life.

One of the areas to which discipline is especially applicable is finances. It is important to create a disciplined budget. I know, I said the 'B' word. Much stress comes to all of us these days due to money, either from the lack of funds or from the inability to handle the funds we have. Being disciplined in the financial areas of your life will give you the freedom to make better choices down the road.

Many people completely misunderstand the purpose of budgeting. They use it as an attempt to allot adequate funds to all areas of financial responsibility in their lives. This is backwards. The process of budgeting (like every other process in this book) is more a tool of evaluation. It is not about giving a little bit of money to every area. It is about deciding what items need to be deleted and what items should have more money allotted to them for long-term use. Budgeting is about dividing items into short-term funds and long-term funds.

Short-term funds consist of money that is used every thirty days. This includes money for groceries, gas, clothes, utilities, and such. This is money you have to use to survive. But, it does not include anything you are making payments on, such as your house, credit cards, cars, boat, and other *assets*. Payments are set up as long-term funds automatically, whether it is for five years or twenty. This is because you have the added weight of interest. The last thing to add to your list is long-term investments. This could be a RRSP, 401k, stocks, or a savings account.

THIS IS WHAT YOUR FORM COULD LOOK LIKE:

SHORT-TERM FUNDS:

Groceries $ _____

Gas (car) $ _____

Utilities $ _____

Cable $ _____

Phone/Cell Phone $ _____

Insurance $ _____

Eating out $ _____

Clothing $ _____

Fees/Memberships (gym etc) $ _____

Misc. (List Separately) $ _____

Gifts/Donations/Church $ _____

LONG-TERM FUNDS

House (own/rent) $ _____

Car (s) $ _____

THE MILLIONAIRE GENIUS

Credit Cards (list sep.) $ _____

Motorcycle/boat payment $ _____

Other installment payment $ _____

LONG-TERM FUNDS (INVESTMENTS)

	Monthly	**Total in Account**
401K / RRSP	$ _____	$ _____
Savings	$ _____	$ _____
College Fund	$ _____	$ _____
Other (stock option etc)	$ _____	$ _____

Your form could be as simple as this, or much more complex. I would encourage you to get your last bank statement and account for every dollar that went out. Many people will assume they spend, say, $100 on eating out, only to find that it is twice that amount or more. Don't assume. Exact figures will help you the most in determining what stays, what goes, and what gets cut back.

This is a necessary process prior to determining what your financial goals will be, so don't gloss this one over. Finances are a big motivator in everything that we do, so take the time and get the correct dollar amounts.

~ *Notes* ~

~ *Notes* ~

~ Notes ~

~ *Notes* ~

CHAPTER FOUR

SUPER ACTION

CHAPTER FOUR

SUPER ACTION

68

> \Pro*cras`ti*na"tion\, n. The act or habit of putting off doing something, especially out of habitual carelessness or laziness.

Research conclusively shows that people must learn to handle procrastination better. Both our own research and that of leading universities indicate that poor time management is a major reason for poor productivity within organizations. In particular, procrastination and unnecessary interruptions top the list of personal productivity killers.

It is relatively easy to come up with excuses for putting things off.

We've probably all used one of the following:

- ♦ I don't have the time right now
- ♦ I'll get around to it later
- ♦ Let me sleep on it first
- ♦ There is lots of time to do that this weekend

It is an epidemic that might have infected you.

WHY DO WE PROCRASTINATE?

The reason is simple: Because we can. It is easy to put off unpleasant, difficult and time-consuming tasks. We end up doing those tasks that scream the loudest. Then, of course, we have to rush to finish them and usually make mistakes in the process. The minute we lick the envelope, we notice we forgot to insert the letter. We start cooking hamburgers only to remember the propane tank on the grill is empty. The good news is that procrastination can be fixed because the problem is easy to pinpoint: It's staring back at you in the mirror!

69

PROCRASTINATION IS A STRANGE PHENOMENON

Procrastination often seems to be a good solution for making life more enjoyable. It accomplishes that by delaying unpleasant responsibilities. But ultimately, procrastination works to make things more difficult and stressful. And it is a rare individual who escapes the dark hand of procrastination. Many people struggle for years to free themselves from its chains in order to forge ahead towards academic success, fulfilling relationships, a clean house, or a muscular body.

Most people understand that they will feel better once their duties are done. But the human brain is infinitely complex, and procrastination easily defeats most of us. It is not necessarily the result of laziness or lack of self-discipline but is often rooted in multiple causes.

> *"Procrastination is the bad habit of putting off until the day after tomorrow what should have been done the day before yesterday. "*
> ~ Napoleon Hill ~

JUST JUMP IN

Get going, even if you have failed in the past. If you want to win you must begin. This seems obvious; but if you have been procrastinating at something, just make a start at it and you will have begun the process of success.

MAKE TIME

Chances are remote that you will ever get anything done without scheduling it. We procrastinate forever because we don't block off the necessary time to finish the job. As we discussed in the last chapter, take the time to evaluate your schedule and make time for your new life.

ONE STEP AT A TIME

You will never start losing weight if you always look at the total amount you need to lose. This makes your goal seem distant and impossible to reach. An alcoholic would have difficulty picturing himself sober for the rest of his/her life. But one can imagine oneself sober for one twenty-four hour period. "One day at a time" is a popular slogan among self-help groups, and for good reason. Don't look at the peak of the mountain and wonder how you will get there. Just put one foot in front of the other and start climbing.

HERE AND NOW

People who conquer procrastination learn to adopt a here-and-now strategy. They never wait until tomorrow to do what they know should be done today. They put things back after each use. They refuse to delay.

FOCUS ON YOUR GOALS

We have already discussed the need for goals in life, but it bears repeating here because it affects the procrastination dilemma. When we set a goal to accomplish something we have already put off and then do it, we take the first step in building a new and powerful habit. Then we must take another step. And then do it again. And again. Repetition of urgency can overcome a life of procrastination. Your need to do things NOW will replace your habit of putting them off.

REFLECT

Those who succeed in life dwell on their successes. Those who are unsuccessful dwell on their failures. It is of great value to remind yourself of areas where you have had successes. While failures seem to stick in the mind longer, if you practice reflecting on your successes on a regular basis the set-backs will fade into the distance.

The really successful people in life have a common denominator: they have mastered their habits. The opposite is true of unsuccessful people. The "under-achievers" have failed because they lack self-discipline. They let things slip. These people seem to have chosen the path of least resistance. They have tried to take the easy way out because it meant less work on the hard things in life, namely to change and control themselves. Who are the most productive and successful people you know? Would they be characterized as people who have mastered themselves? Are they highly disciplined people?

PUTTING OFF A LITTLE TO GET A LOT

This is the idea of delaying the reward or pleasure from doing something in order to enjoy bigger benefits later. It's getting the unpleasant task done first to enjoy the gratification more deeply at a future date.

THE MILLIONAIRE GENIUS

How far would basketball superstar Shaquille O'Neal get if he tried to put the blessing or victory phase before the workout or investment phase? In a game, he wouldn't go very far without the endurance training and late-night practices. There's no way he could handle the game without delaying certain pleasures in order to enjoy the victory phase later.

Delayed gratification means working on problems NOW and enjoying the benefits of solving the problem later. It may be tough, but we'd all agree that to really enjoy the pleasure of the payoff phase you must first do the hard work. You forego small rewards now so you can benefit greatly later.

Most people wish for more self discipline. Many times a day you may think critically of yourself for postponing things that you know you want to change. There are certain things you know you should stop doing, yet you never seem to tackle them quickly. There are habits you know you should start mastering, but haven't begun.

The psychological cost for living this way is huge. You know exactly what you need to do. For some reason, perhaps lack of motivation, lack of initiative, or lack of a plan, you have permitted yourself and your life to become cluttered with undesirable habits. The time to change all that is now.

My contention is that most people already know what they need to do to earn more money, have better relationships, and enjoy better physical health and emotional well-being. The problem lies not in knowing what to do. It lies much more with doing what we know we should.

THE 6-STEP PROCESS FOR DEVELOPING DISCIPLINE IN YOUR LIFE

STEP 1: DEFINE PURPOSE.

Identify one habit or area in life in which you would like more discipline. The first step is to identify one specific behavior you would like to change. It should be written in specific behavioral language. It should describe something you do that you would like to stop doing, or something you don't do consistently and would like to do regularly.

You can use this step to describe the outcome(s) you would like to accomplish. You must, however, confine each worksheet to one specific issue or behavior. Attempting to do too much may be discouraging. Each worksheet will take you through this 6-Step process. It only applies to one issue per worksheet.

STEP 2: FIND ROLE MODELS.

Ask yourself, "Who is doing it right?" By identifying one or more people who have discipline in this area, you will see that if others can do it, so can you. The people you list in this section need not be personal acquaintances of yours. You may not know them personally at all. They may be alive or dead. The point here is to cause you to think about specific people who you believe had control in this area. These are the people you will emulate.

STEP 3: SEE SUCCESS

Now ask yourself, "What's in it for me?" You want to consider why you want to develop in this area. By listing the rewards you will be willing to work harder. You need to hear, smell, taste, see, and touch exactly what it will be once you are strong in this area. This step gets you focused on the benefits of self-discipline. You might also consider listing the pain of NOT becoming disciplined here.

STEP 4: DELAY GRATIFICATION

You now need to consider where you might fail, or identify the danger zones. You know that if you are going to become more disciplined you will be tempted to fall off the wagon, to be led astray, and to procrastinate. If you have been attempting to become more self-disciplined for some time, then you know there is a pattern to the failure. What happens for you? You start off strongly, then before you know it, you are doing the very things you said you wouldn't, or you have stopped doing the things you said you would.

73

List all the potential times, situations, and areas that may cause you to fall, and then list how you will handle each of them. If you know that on business trips you eat too much, consider this a danger zone. By acknowledging it, you can plan on how to handle it.

STEP 5: USE ADVANCED DECISION-MAKING

You cannot win in life if you are controlled by whimsical or situational decision-making. If you are to succeed in life, you will need to consider in advance how you will live your life.

In this step you will need to give some thought to what specific actions you will need to take to accomplish the goal listed in Step 1. For example, if you wanted to become more disciplined in the area of exercise, one decision made in advance could be a decision to exercise every morning, upon waking, for 45 minutes while watching a video workout tape. Advanced Decision-Making says: "It's already been decided. I live my life based on decisions made in advance. The decision cannot, will not be reversed." You decide in advance that you will do this. You don't wait until the morning to see if you "feel" like doing it. You have already decided in advance how you will live your life.

STEP 6: ENROLL A SUPPORT TEAM.

This step is by far one of the most crucial. If you don't do this step, you are cheating yourself out of the real power behind this system. It is vital for you in order to become the strong and self-disciplined person you know you can and should be. Resist the temptation to avoid this step out of discomfort. Following it will literally change your life.

What this step asks you to do is enlist the assistance of someone you respect to help you become disciplined in this area. Here's what you do: First, you need to think of someone whom you respect and someone who will be strong enough to hold you to certain decisions about becoming disciplined. You call this person and tell them that you are involved in this material and you have identified certain areas in which you desire more discipline. You are going to send him a copy of the worksheet, and you would like him to hold you accountable to the actions and decisions on the sheet.

This activity forces you to do what you said you would do. Find someone to call you at least once a week. Allow yourself to become accountable to this person.

AVOID THE THREE LIES.

Every time a person breaks a commitment and falls back into a bad habit, he has bought into one of the three lies of the Habit Demons. Think back to when you started a bad habit. Think about what happens to every alcoholic who falls off the wagon, or to people who gain back the weight they lost, or someone who wastes piles of time dealing with issues she once had under control. These three lies rear their ugly heads; we believe them, and then we fall prey to them.

LIE #1: "ONCE WILL BE ENOUGH"

"Just have one beer, one smoke, one dessert." Anytime you hear something inside yourself that sounds like this it's lie #1. Is one beer enough for an alcoholic? No, one is too many, and a thousand are not enough. Whenever you hear "once" or "just this time," let a red flag remind you about the Habit Demons' lies.

LIE #2: "MESS IT UP GOOD"

Once you give in to Lie #1 and do something you know you shouldn't, then Lie #2 kicks in. "Now that you've blown it, mess it up good." It looks like this for someone trying to control the bad habit of eating late at night. "Just have one piece of pie. One little piece can't hurt you. You deserve just one small piece." So you start cutting yourself a piece. Soon afterwards you hear Lie #2. "Well, now you've done it. You might as well have another piece now. Wouldn't another piece taste great? You've blown it, so why not mess it up good? Go ahead, have another piece and why not top it off with some vanilla ice cream?" So you give in and feel terrible. Then comes Lie #3, which is the final stage of loss of control.

LIE #3: "GIVE UP"

By giving in and doing what you did not want to do, you feel terrible. You have "messed it up good," so now the natural progression is to stop trying; in other words, you simply "give up." What this lie tries to get you to say is, "I'm worthless, I'm hopeless, I will never be able to control my habits. I'll quit trying."

76

Reject all three lies; they are false. Doing something once is rarely enough. If you are tempted to do something wrong "once," see if it's not lie #1. If you do mess something up, don't mess it up worse. You don't have to go any further. You can resume control. Exercise that control now. Never believe Lie #3, never quit trying. You are of immense value, and you are never hopeless.

> *"You control your future, your destiny. What you think about comes about. By recording your dreams and goals on paper, you set in motion the process of becoming the person you most want to be. Put your future in good hands – your own. "*
>
> ~ Mark Victor Hansen ~

~ *Notes* ~

~ *Notes* ~

~ Notes ~

~ *Notes* ~

CHAPTER FIVE

SUPER GOALS

CHAPTER FIVE

SUPER GOALS

You probably have been setting goals since you were a young child. It is natural for children to dream about what they will be when they grow up. They imagine themselves as astronauts or ballerinas. A child is not born fearful. A child believes that all things are possible. So what happened? Why do we lose this belief as we age?

Our dreams are tempered many times by those around us, especially by those in authority. When we are little, those in positions of authority over us smile indulgently at our dreams, but as we get older they will often admonish us to be more "realistic." Unfortunately, they use the idea of reality in the wrong way. Truly, as we grow, we have unlimited potential. So the reality they speak of is *their* vision of *your* future. It is reality based on *their* experiences, though none of those have happened to *you* yet. They fear seeing you fail because of the disappointment they felt over their own failures, so they admonish you to dull down your dreams and live within *their* ideas of what is possible.

As an adult you can tap back into those dreams that you have pushed aside or hidden, and now you have the added advantage of wisdom. You know that while you can learn from your past experiences and the experiences of those around you, it does not mean that you will have a similar outcome.

Rather than pursue a goal or dream, many people take what is at hand and try to form a happy life from their circumstances. They don't strive toward what they really want or toward what they can really create, they only muddle through with what they are given. This can happen with your job, your relationships, and even your health; and if you don't pay attention it happens before you even realize it.

Goal-setting can be a tricky business. While you don't want to be completely off the charts into fantasyland, you also don't want to set your sights too low. Otherwise you will spend your life underachieving, and even if you reach every low goal you set you will always wonder "what if?"

We have spent half of this book uncovering your core attitudes and beliefs and figuring out what paradigms you want to change. Now all of the information you have been writing down will come into play as you decide what *you really want*. And I say "really" because no one is going to give you everything you want just because you decide you want it. You will have to work for it, sacrifice for it, and be willing to put in one-hundred percent of yourself towards it, no matter what obstacles stand in your way.

Writing down these goals is an important part of the process. Though many people set goals once a year, at New Year's or on their birthdays for example, they usually shove them in a drawer and don't even look at them until the next year. But even they are way ahead of almost everyone else, all those who just take life as it comes and hope for the best. I ask you, though, hope for what? That it won't be horrific? A good life takes active planning and active participation, and even if you're the once-a-year kind of goal setter then that's better than nothing. But in order to move forward as quickly as possible, it pays to revisit your goals on a weekly and monthly basis. Then, at the end of the year, you can be pleasantly shocked at how far you've come in such a short time, rather than feeling depressed at having the same exact goals for the next year because you didn't get anywhere.

There is one thing you must understand about setting goals. They are as rewarding as they are risky. There is the chance that you will fail. You must understand that on day one and plan in your mind how you will react if your first step toward your goal doesn't work out. Will you quit? Or will you push forward and believe in yourself?

What makes a good goal? Even if you have an idea at this point of what you want, how do you write that down in a way that will be achievable? An effective goal has certain identifiable elements, which include the following:

1. Clear and specifically defined
2. Achievable in the given timeframe
3. Measurable
4. Aligned with other short-term or long-term goals
5. Flexible in terms of acceleration or escalation

Let's take the first one, "clear and specifically defined." You might say to yourself, "I want to retire at forty-five," or, "I want to never have to worry about money." While those are great ideas, they aren't specific enough, so you don't know how you are doing on the plan. You must have a means of gauging whether you are falling behind, or moving ahead of where you should be. A better way to phrase this goal might be, "I want to make X number of dollars so I can retire at forty-five and not worry about money."

Most people respond better to very specific goals than they do to vague terms such as "do better" or "be the best." Specific goals will give you a target to shoot at so you get some sense of how far you have to go and how fast you have to travel. A good goal will tell you how, when, where, and by what means so you can track your progress.

> *"Just as your car runs more smoothly and requires less energy to go faster and farther when the wheels are in perfect alignment, you perform better when your thoughts, feelings, emotions, goals, and values are in balance."*
>
> ~ Brian Tracy ~

Let's take the retirement goal again. If you are going to make, let's say, two million dollars and retire by the age of forty-five, then you need to list possibilities. They might include: putting a specific dollar amount (or percentage of income) into an investment account every month, or getting a job that pays X amount per year, getting a higher education and leveraging that into a higher career path, and doubling your income in five years. Here's an example:

Jerry, a fifty-three year old attorney, had been setting goals for years, but he didn't know how to do it effectively.

"Every year for over ten years I'd set the same two goals: to stop smoking and to lose weight. Twelve months later I'd put on more weight and was smoking more heavily. I really did want to change, but it seemed like an overwhelming job because I didn't know how to break it down into doable goals and tasks. One year I set my usual goals, but then I also added some sub-goals. I decided I'd smoke one cigarette less each day until I was out. It worked. I was smoke-free within a month. So then I tried it on my weight, which had increased even more when I stopped smoking. I set goals of walking every day and cutting back on snacks and soft drinks. Within a month I'd lost ten pounds. Meeting that goal encouraged me to set an even bigger and better goal the next month. By the time New Year's rolled around, I'd been smoke free for eleven months and had lost almost forty pounds. Though I'd tried for years, I didn't understand that having a clear step-by-step path was the way to go. It is amazing what you can achieve if you just work at it a little bit each day."

One thing I would caution you not to do is to confuse goals and tasks. Goals are the big targets, and tasks are the small stepping stones that get you there. For example, if your goal is to get a new job then a task might be sending out resumes to prospective employers. Doing small tasks toward your goal every day is important because it gives you a sense of control and accomplishment. However, be sure that all the small tasks are working towards the goal. It is very easy to seem busy when, in truth, you aren't really getting anywhere. Write down each activity you perform on the path to your goal and evaluate it on a weekly or monthly basis. This will tell you if you are spending too much time on things that aren't moving you forward.

SHORT-TERM AND LONG-TERM GOALS

Everyone needs both short and long-term goals. Some short-term goals are based on a sense of urgency; for example, "Lose ten pounds before my daughter's wedding in six weeks." Others are stepping stones to reach your long-term goals, as in, "Take three night classes this semester towards getting my degree."

So why not just make the big long-term goals and do away with all these short-term goals? Humans perform better with regular and consistent reinforcement. As you track your progress and see how many short-term goals you have accomplished, it makes the long-term goals seem that much closer and easier to reach.

Long-term goals have a very important function as well. In addition to giving you an overall direction, they also provide a focal point when times get hard or when you suffer setbacks in your short-term goals. Focusing on the long-term goals and being able to see the big picture can get you through those times when it would be easier to quit. You will be able to see your situation as temporary and to reinforce your will to search for solutions. As you overcome each difficulty, your renewed focus builds the confidence you will need to push on toward that long-term goal.

So how do you start setting your goals? I have designed a worksheet that will help you focus on your life goals and teach you how to break them down into bite-sized chunks. Then we will further break them down into individual tasks. You will want to alter this form to suit your own timetable and goals, but you must write them down and track them. I'm going to use a few examples for this worksheet so you can see how it flows.

GOAL WORKSHEET

LONG-TERM GOAL:
I. Make at least $100,000 per year

A. SHORT-TERM GOALS RELATED TO LONG-TERM GOAL
1. Seek promotion with current employer

2. Learn to invest in real estate

3. Start my own business part-time

You can see how the long-term goals and short-term goals are interrelated. You will go through this process for each life goal you have and create a similar list. You can do this for any area of your life. Here is another example:

LONG-TERM GOAL:
II. Lose 50 Pounds and Run a 10K

A. SHORT-TERM GOALS RELATED TO LONG-TERM GOAL
1. Lose 3 pounds per week

2. Start exercising at least three times each week

THE MILLIONAIRE GENIUS

Once you have several life goals laid out in this fashion, you can develop a task list. This is a weekly or monthly list of tasks related to each long-term goal. For the two examples above, it might look something like this:

Life Goal #1 – Earn $100,000 per year

Task list:

1. See what positions are available or might be coming available with my employer.

2. Sit down with my boss and ask if there are any ways for me to improve or expand my job skills. Indicate that I'm willing to do whatever it takes to get the job done.

3. Ask friends for referrals to realtors that have experience with real estate investments. Request a lunch meeting to discuss the pros and cons. Also ask if they can put me in touch with someone who is already familiar with real estate investing who might act as a mentor.

4. Evaluate my current job skills and see if there are any opportunities for consulting work or other entrepreneurial options that could produce additional income.

Life Goal #2 – Lose 50 Pounds and Run a 10K

Task list:

1. Schedule visit with doctor to discuss effective diet plans. Get a good physical so I have a defined starting point and can track my progress.

2. Join a gym and go at least three times a week.

3. Schedule a meeting with a personal trainer to discuss the planned 10K run and get a workout regime that will provide the right conditioning.

4. Attend a 10K and get inspired. Talk with some of the runners and ask their advice for training, etc.

89

You can see that concentrating on your life goals will make you a very busy person. This is why it was essential to sit down and clear things off your current schedule. In order to get where you want to be, you must allow time to work on your goals. Otherwise, you will never move forward at all.

I still track all my own goals on a daily basis. It's not something you eventually finish or get to the end of. Goal setting is a life-long positive force that you learn and consistently work on. My goals are set up in my planner that I add tasks to every day. I evaluate my progress on a monthly basis and formulate a plan to work on for the next month. There is a natural ebb and flow to the goal worksheets. Sometimes one goal moves ahead at lightning speed, while another trudges along at a snail's pace. But I can see each month that all are moving forward. This gives me great motivation to continue. It also acts as a red flag if I slack off and don't do much toward a particular goal. I can see instantly that if I only completed one or two tasks related to that goal for the month, then any expectation of great forward strides is unrealistic. You get out of life what you put into it, and seeing it in black and white terms keeps you from lying to yourself or procrastinating.

Procrastination is a big wrecking ball when it comes to goal-setting. This is why so many people get to the end of the year and realize that the New Year's resolution they made last year didn't budge an inch. They put off working on it each week, then each month, until another whole year has passed. Time is a thief, and procrastination is its accomplice. The world keeps moving forward, whether you do or not, and by standing still you get left further and further behind.

Setting goals can be very motivating. But in order to sustain that motivation you have to choose goals that are within your realm of control and within a doable timetable. What does this mean? Let's say you decide that you want to make a million dollars and have a record deal in a year. While you may be able to accomplish both of these goals in the long-term, the timetable of a year is probably unrealistic. You have to have certain skills to accomplish both of these goals. One of the reasons I used the example of increasing income to $100,000 with no timeline is that the timeline will vary, depending on where you start. If you are making minimum wage and have no education, you will need to work harder and longer than someone who is already making $40,000 per year with a bachelor's degree. You will also know that some of the first tasks I listed toward this goal are to find people who are investing in real estate and get advice and training.

If I had listed as one of the first tasks to get a loan and invest in real estate with no background or knowledge, then that would be completely unrealistic and even dangerous. You must be willing to ask questions, learn the area of your interest thoroughly, and find people who can help you. This will move you toward your goal quickly and with much less risk than simply beginning with no knowledge or training. This is one reason the short-term goals and task list are so important. They force you to really think through the process of getting to your goal and to focus on the details of getting from point A to point B. You know up front how much time and effort it will take and can adjust your goals accordingly.

Just like it is unrealistic to think you can lose fifty pounds in a month and keep them off, it is also unrealistic to think you can make a million dollars in a year and have any idea how to keep the money and invest it correctly. You have to put in the time to learn, and it will pay off for you in the end.

While it may seem that all this planning and thinking about your goals is wasting time that you could spend achieving them, it is not. Remember I said that knowing what not to do is almost as important as knowing what to do. By learning, especially from others and from mentors, you save time because you are helping yourself to avoid the pitfalls they experienced. Every setback you can avoid is time saved toward achieving your long-term goal.

Here's an example of unnecessary setbacks that could have been avoided. Jenny and Jeff have invested in real estate for the past fifteen years and made many mistakes. Jeff tells the story:

> *"We started investing in rental property when our kids were young. We decided that in order to have Jenny stay home with the boys and still save for college and meet our expenses, we needed something flexible that produced income. Since Jenny had an accounting background it seemed like a natural thing for her to be involved in. We started with a couple of properties and got a crash course in what not to do. We bought houses that were in bad shape and rented them to the wrong people. We ended up spending more money on repairs and expenses than we made. Jenny still had to work full time, plus we both spent our weekends managing the problems in the houses or trying to fix them ourselves.*

> *"It got so bad we felt like we were just throwing money away hand over fist and not making anything. I was complaining to my brother one day about the mess we were in, and he suggested I go talk to a real estate broker who had been investing in his own properties for years. I did, and he showed us what we had done wrong and gave us the steps we needed to take to fix our errors and make our real estate profitable. It took us five years to get things on track and really make money. Now the boys are in college, and we have a great income from our properties. But it took us five years of financial nightmare before we got our heads above water.*

"If we had taken the time to sit down with someone who had experience before we jumped into real estate, we could have saved ourselves years of worry and struggle, not to mention thousands of dollars. If I have any advice for anyone, it is to do your home work and save the heartache."

Many obstacles can and will get in your way as you strive toward your goals. But studying where you want to go and how you are going to get there gives you a clear path and helps you avoid problems.

The flip side of setting unrealistic goals is to set life goals that are too low, or really should be short-term goals. Something that is easily attainable hardly qualifies as a goal at all. Try not to underestimate yourself or discount the skills you have. As a general rule, people become easily bored with a goal that is too easy. They lose interest, and you will too.

You must pick goals that challenge you professionally, mentally, and even spiritually. Go for things that make you stretch your possibilities and require high levels of creativity and energy to meet. You will never achieve great things without pushing yourself. Goals that don't push you will move you sideways, not forward. They do not get you out of your comfort zone or force you to learn new and difficult things. It takes two key factors to reach any goal, seriousness and flexibility.

Being serious about a goal means that you take the necessary steps to achieve it. It is focusing on the goals and how to accomplish them. As you develop your task list, this becomes your working strategy of how you are going to accomplish your goal. You are giving yourself self-imposed deadlines for specific tasks and evaluating your own progress. You are then developing the next set of strategic tasks to move forward. The first step to being serious is to write down your goals. The second step is to announce it publicly. This may seem like you are giving those around you the opportunity to ridicule you in advance, and some may. But by first writing your goal down and then announcing it you now have additional motivation, since you know people will be asking about your progress. This makes you accountable not only to yourself but also to others.

You have probably heard people close to you announce their plans, but how did they do it? Did they say, "I'm going to lose fifty pounds and run a 10K by this time next year," or did they say something like, "After the holidays I'm going to lose weight, and then I'll be able to do what I want"?

If I heard someone make the first statement, I would assume that he was serious and committed to his goals. However, If I heard the second statement I would wonder how serious he was, if this was just a hope that he didn't really plan to work toward. Whenever I hear phrases like, "I hope to …/I'd like to …/Someday I will …" I always feel a sense of disappointment. This person, instead of setting a goal and being willing to work hard to get what he wants, is content to just wish and daydream. Here again, procrastination is a goal killer. If you are thinking that you will start after the holidays, on your birthday, or after such and so happens, you are just wishing, too. Every day you waste is a day wasted. You don't get it back, and you don't get to do it over, so get busy.

The second key factor to reaching your goal is flexibility. This does not mean giving yourself a break and being lazy. This means using creativity in overcoming obstacles and listening to feedback. This will help you fine-tune your goals as you go. You must have the ability to step back on a regular basis (I recommend at least monthly) and evaluate your progress. What worked? What didn't? What changes are you going to make in your strategy and task list for next month?

Remember that we said that goal-setting involves risk. That means risking a wrong move, bad decision, and even a major setback. It also means that you must be adaptable to changing circumstances. You must still juggle performing your job, providing for your family, and paying your bills in addition to striving toward your goals. There are times when certain goals will temporarily take a backseat, but all of these instances will give you the opportunity to be creative and perhaps even to come up with another opportunity that fits into your long-term goals.

Joe was a hospital billing clerk who desperately wanted to make more money and run his own business.

"My wife Ann and I have four kids. They were all young then, and we were struggling financially. The kids were all involved in soccer, baseball, tennis, you name it. I set my goals but realized that I spent so much time running from event to event that I didn't have anytime to pursue my goals. I couldn't give up the time with my kids, so I felt stuck.

"One day, on the way home from a soccer game, I stopped and got the kids a snow cone at a little roadside stand. An elderly man named Ronny ran the place, and we started talking. He told me how he used to have his stand on wheels so he could make all the soccer games, but his health had declined and he didn't have the energy to do it anymore. It sparked an idea. With Ronny's help and advice, the kids and I bought a used trailer and converted it into a rolling snow cone stand. Ronny helped us get the necessary approvals and permits for our city, and we took our trailer to all the games selling snow cones to the crowd.

"The kids pitched in and took turns working the stand with my wife and me so we could watch the other kids play. It was great family time because we were all working together and making money. By the time the kids were in high school we had four trailers making hundreds of games around the city every summer.

"I often wonder what our lives would have been like if I hadn't stopped at Ronny's stand that day twenty years ago. It's amazing how focusing on your goals can make you see opportunities that were probably always there."

Once you have started on your journey toward your life goals, you must be willing to seek out critical feedback and be receptive to it. Feedback is important because no matter how well you have researched or planned, there will always be some areas that you have overlooked or were unaware of. You may also lose your perspective from time to time and may be unable to assess your own efforts correctly. At those times a wise or experienced friend or mentor can help you get back on track.

Friends and advisors who are aware of your pursuit will also be able to offer encouragement. Many times as you become immersed in pursuing your goal you may find that you also become lonely. You are choosing to travel a new direction from others who have been in your life, and they may be a little bit distant. Your friends and mentors can offer feedback and give you a morale boost when you need it. Talk to them about where you are on the path to your goals, what progress you've made, and what problems you have encountered. They may be able to offer suggestions or solutions as well.

A good example of the kind of mental struggle you may go through is losing weight. If you hop on the scale every day and obsess over every ounce gained or lost, then it becomes easy to let your sense of perspective get out of whack. Before you started, a two pound weight gain might have been no big deal, but now it feels like a crushing blow. Talking with your mentor or a friend will remind you how far you've come, and that you need to step back and stop obsessing. Being overly "anal" (mired in details) or obsessively focused will end up frustrating and hurting your attempt to pursue your goals.

Reassess your efforts no more than once a week at the most; monthly is better. Reshape your strategic tasks regularly, and be flexible and creative with solutions.

OTHER GOALS

So by now you've written down your long-term and short-term goals. But what about those goals that don't really fit anywhere? The ones like fixing up the spare bedroom and repainting the den? On my personal goal planner I have another category; it is called "Other" and contains all my miscellaneous goals. These are usually ultra short-term goals I want to accomplish. By ultra short I mean things I intend to accomplish in less than a year. For you these might include getting the dog house-trained, finding an apartment closer to work, or redoing the den. Learning a foreign language or learning how to paint might also go on this list.

These tend to be less involved and pressing, but if they are important enough to write down they still need to get done. They also provide a sense of accomplishment and improved quality of life. You know those twenty little honey-dos that you have needed to get done? Put them on your task list and start doing them one at a time. It is easier and less overwhelming than trying to get them all done in a weekend. Just start on the list and work as far as you can. By taking care of little issues you can also improve your home life and gain support for yourself as you work toward your bigger goals.

DOUBTS

I'd be lying if I said I didn't have any doubts along the way. We all have doubts and suffer the occasional crises of faith in ourselves and our abilities. These can be compounded by family and friends who may be telling you everything that you can't do and discouraging you from moving forward. You have to remember to focus on your plan. This means not letting your emotions get the best of you to the point that you try to "prove everyone wrong." While harsh comments may motivate you to strive toward your goal, they may also lead you into the pit of self-sabotage. When you allow others to affect your plan and you try to accelerate it to prove something, you can end up with less than you started with.

For example, let's say you want to write a novel in a year. You plan to go to conferences, take classes, and spend your evenings and weekends pursuing this goal. When you tell your friends and family about your plan, you hear, "You don't have the stamina to write a whole novel! What are you thinking?" This could prompt you to resolve to prove them wrong immediately. So you sit down and try to write the book in a few days. You discover that there is much you don't know and much you need to learn in order to finish. You become discouraged and give up. Rather than sticking to your plan to learn first, you jumped in and failed. Your family's prediction has become self fulfilling.

You must guard yourself against this kind of reaction. Stick to your plan and avoid the traps. We talked in the previous chapters about being able to forgive yourself. If you blow it, start again. Build on what you have and learn from each lesson. One of Newton's laws of physics is, "An object in motion tends to remain in motion, while an object at rest tends to remain at rest." This captures the physical phenomenon of "inertia." The same is true for the human mind. If you feel in control and like you are making progress, then it is easier to keep going. However, if you feel out of control and come to a stop, then it takes even more effort to get going again. You are most certainly your worst critic. Leave your mistakes in the past and continue to move forward.

We also talked in a previous chapter about visualizing your goal. Remember, Chris's coach did this with the basketball team by taking them to the state tournament and then having them sit for five minutes before every practice and encouraging them to imagine what it would be like to play there. Visualization can play an important part in maintaining your focus and motivating you toward your goal. Now that you have your goals written down, you can visualize what it would be like to reach those goals.

For example, let's say that you and your wife have decided to plan a once-in–a-lifetime family vacation to Hawaii. You allow yourself eighteen months to save the money and make arrangements. To encourage the whole family to pitch in and make the necessary financial sacrifices, you visit a travel agent and get brochures and flyers showing the beautiful islands. You put these up on the wall so everyone can see them. At least once a month you encourage your family to talk about the upcoming vacation, what they want to see or do and how they imagine it will be. You watch educational shows on the cultural and geological history of the area. You occasionally plan a Hawaiian dinner and let the kids help in preparing exotic foods.

There are many more things you can do as well. While it may seem silly to some, this will allow your entire family to visualize this fabulous trip and anticipate being there. They will be excited and anxious and will help you make this goal happen. And, more importantly, they will take on responsibility and ownership to **make** it happen. Rather than spending a stressful eighteen months full of money battles and arguments, you will have eighteen months full of anticipation and excitement and a much easier time getting everyone to work toward a common goal.

To learn other powerful ways to create your goals and have a system that will allow you to attract these goals into your life. Check out **www.MillionaireGenius.com** and attend one of my live seminar or teleconferences events.

"A goal is a dream with a deadline."
~ Napoleon Hill ~

~ *Notes* ~

~ *Notes* ~

~ Notes ~

~ *Notes* ~

CHAPTER SIX

Super Networking

CHAPTER SIX

SUPER NETWORKING

Take a look at the personal goal sheets you compiled from the last chapter. Are there goals concerning money? Retiring early? Providing well for your family? You may also have some goals that include owning your own business, creating a new product or relating your own life experiences to others. So how do we share these goals with others? And how do we find the help we need to pursue them?

As humans, we do have the ability to get by on our own resources, but most of us do not want to act alone. We are social animals, and as such we constantly exchange our experiences and knowledge with those around us. It is what has helped us to survive! Think about it this way: When you want to look for a new job, whom do you ask first? You probably answered, "Friends and family." Do they know of any openings where they work? Studies have shown that most people rely on information from other people to find jobs. This reliance on communication from those we love is most evident when there is a threat or crisis. How many times have you called for medical advice from your mother when your child was sick? How often have you seen a disaster on television and picked up the phone to make sure your relatives were safe?

We also talk to make sense of the things we experience. Years ago I had a friend who worked in a small coffee shop. He told me that farmers would come in every morning and talk about their timing of the planting, the weather conditions, and the newest farm bill that was before Congress. Their talk accomplished two goals. First, they shared any new or current information they had with the others; and second, they discussed the best course of action given the circumstances. They shared information and made sense of their world. Like these farmers, people in the workplace form networking groups to share information and decide on actions.

One of the most important reasons we talk is to reduce risk, uncertainty, and costs. This goes along with what the farmers talked about each morning and is one of the reasons I encourage you to find a mentor for any new business endeavor. You will have someone to be a sounding board for your ideas so you can reduce the risk and uncertainty. We do this every day, almost without thought. If you have to switch doctors, you don't go to the phone book unless you don't know anyone with your particular health issue. Most of us ask people. If you are looking to buy a new car you talk to friends and family about their cars and experiences with them. You don't want to have a poor product or service, and you certainly don't want to pay too much. Generally speaking, the younger you are the more important it is to engage in this kind of information gathering, and the more important it is to rely on the feedback you receive.

We also talk to entertain and to relieve tension. How many times have you told ghost stories at a campfire or laughed about old memories with a spouse or long time friend to get through a tough day? As you have read through this book, there has been a mix of solid facts and ideas as well as real life examples. Those examples are necessary in order to help you receive the message I'm trying to send. This is an important fact to remember when you are trying to get your own message across to others. How can you get them to relate to you and understand where you are coming from? By giving them a glimpse of the real you and allowing them to follow along as you relate your triumphs and tragedies.

> *"Networking is an essential part of building wealth."*
> ~ Armstrong Williams ~

105

This means you must empathize with others; empathy is the only truly human emotion. An animal can love and feel pain and loss, but it cannot empathize. Animals live in the moment; they don't cry when they see a dog hit by a car on television. They don't rejoice when they witness a soldier coming home safe and unharmed. Humans do. And that is because we have the ability to put ourselves in another person's place for a short time and feel the same emotions as those who are directly involved. We empathize with how they feel even if the people we are watching are merely actors on a stage.

You must also use these genuine emotions in your attitude towards yourself and your goals. Just as you want to communicate self-confidence to your friends and family, you must have the attitude of success and believe passionately and wholeheartedly in what you are doing. You must set your goals and have the strength to move toward them in an efficient and consistent manner. And then you must convince others. This is where the idea of word of mouth helps you.

Let's take the example of wanting to learn more about real estate investing. You get to know a broker who can teach you about the business and also introduce you to others. He introduces you to several realtors and a couple of other investors who are doing the same thing.

Make no mistake, these people will watch you very closely for any clue that you may not be serious or sincere. If they sense for one second that you are looking for an easy buck or are not willing to put in the time to learn, then don't expect them to return your calls. How you present yourself to your new contacts and connections is vital if you really want to reach your goals.

Once they have seen you in action and know that you are sincere, they will take your education in the business up a level. They will share secrets that they would never divulge to an insincere beginner. This will speed you ahead on your path and increase your income much faster than if you tried to begin by yourself. These initial networking contacts may also become potential business partners and co-investors at some point, so you must never underestimate the power of their opinions.

1. Are you willing to put the same time and effort into a new area of business that you have in real estate (or whatever business you are currently in)?

2. Are you willing to put off your ultimate goals and split your time?

3. Do you have a mentor or contact other than the person offering the opportunity that you could get advice and help from?

4. Is the person offering the opportunity an expert, and is he or she willing to work at the same level you have to achieve his or her dreams?

By increasing your circle of contacts, you become a connection point for more and more like-minded people. You may be presented with a number of other opportunities for investment and gain, but you must be very careful about which ones you choose. If your expertise and focus is going to be real estate, then what do you do if a friend or colleague offers you half ownership in a restaurant? While you may be thinking, "Great! I love to eat," you must also realize that this could be potential trouble. You don't know anything about the restaurant business. So what questions do you ask yourself to know if you should take this chance or not? Below is a short list of things to consider:

You must take all of these factors into consideration. On the surface, I would immediately say no to this deal. It's out of your area of expertise and will drain your energy and resources from your main goal. Now if this had been an experienced real estate investor looking for a partner to buy an apartment complex, then that is another story entirely. You already know the experts you will need to talk to, and it is within you realm of expertise. It ADDS to what you are doing rather than taking you in a whole different direction.

107

Let's look at another example in a completely different area. Let's say that you want to write a book. It may be to convey a true story of an event in your life, a memoir, or even a work of fiction. It could also be a book about how you reached your own goals and now want to help other do the same. You don't need a degree in English to write a book, but you do need to be willing to learn. Take a class or two from your local college and go to a writing conference or two. Why? To meet published authors, because these are the people who will be your mentors. They can steer you in the right direction, introduce you to the right people, and put you on the fast track toward publication. Here again you must have the attitude of success and an absolutely unshakable faith in your goal. Once your book is written, other authors are a good source of feedback. They can suggest improvements for your manuscript and offer suggestions and markets for the work.

Once published, you must look at your book as your product. You want to get people talking about it. There are numerous ways to do this, including offering your services as a speaker for civic groups and conferences. This gives you the opportunity to talk to many people at once and also to sell copies of your book. These people will read and talk. And talk. And talk.

While it may seem like you would do better by investing in lots of advertising, the opposite is true where books are concerned. People recommend books based on their own experiences. This is why reviews of books and movies are so important. It gives the public a good idea of what someone they look up to thinks of the work. If you give them a good story and are someone that the reviewers and audience can identify with, then you may go on to be a best-selling author. But it doesn't happen overnight or without great effort on your part.

Both of these examples require you to have the ability to network effectively with others. This means that you must cultivate the ability to meet and connect with numerous people in a short time and maintain those connections.

You have to think of the people you know as you own personal spider web. Some are closer (friends and family), and others are more distant (co-workers and acquaintances). You must work as the spider does to add more and more rings to your own personal web. Most people know an average of about 250 people. These are friends, relatives, co-workers past and present, neighbors, church friends, former school mates, etc. Now if you know 250 people, and they each know 250 people, and they each know 250 people, then you see where this is going. You increase your ability to influence the people you know exponentially with every new contact, friend, and business acquaintance you meet. Each time you interact with someone new, a door of opportunity is opened to perhaps thousands of new people. This network of people increases your leverage in the business world and opens countless doors. It brings new customers merely by people in your network talking to people in theirs.

One misconception that most people have about their networks is that it is those who are the closest who are the most beneficial. In fact, just the opposite is true. Those you have weak ties to often can produce more networking connections than those closest to you. The reason is that the people closest to you have many of the same contacts in common. They don't know that many people who don't already know you. But your acquaintances and co-workers come from all walks of life and all different areas of the country. They will have a completely different set of people to influence and give you more leverage in the long run.

It is a learned skill to seek out and maintain active ties with your weak contacts. You must put forth the effort to maintain the relationship. One way to do this is to offer something free that is of value to that network of people. Let's go back to the book example. If you agree to speak at a writer's conference for free or for little pay they are not only grateful but they will also allow you access to their entire network. This network becomes a whole group of individuals that you can now call acquaintances. You can offer more to these acquaintances by suggesting they sign up for your e-mail newsletter. This maintains the contact, and rather than just forgetting about you in a week or two they are receiving a good, useful newsletter from you each month. You should strive each day to make new contacts and do whatever is necessary to maintain them. They are extremely valuable to your future success.

Most people have some vague idea that networking and word-of-mouth are extremely important in building a business or advancing your goals, but most have no idea how to get it started. I've been there myself, standing in my living room looking out my front picture window. I know the people are there. I know they will want what I have to give. How do I reach them? Where do I start?

I have boiled the process of expanding your network and increasing word of mouth down to a few simple steps. You must remember that these steps are only a starting point, and you can add to or adjust them as you go.

Network Building 101

1. Assess what you have. Write down a list of every single person that you know, have been introduced to, or are acquainted with. These individuals will become your initial contact base. This is time consuming but important. Shoot for at least 200-300 names.

2. Look at those already around you. There are people you pass in the hallway, sit next to on the train, and go to church with all the time that you have never met. Make a list of organizations and groups that you belong to. How many members are there in each organization? Can some of the people you already know give you an introduction to these people you don't know yet? Concentrate on meeting at least one or two new people per day.

3. Consider new prospects. Are there other organizations or opportunities that could give you exposure to large numbers of people in a short amount of time. Like the example of speaking at a conference, look for opportunities where you can offer something valuable to the members of organizations you haven't been familiar with in the past.

4. Make use of the Internet. It almost goes without saying that you need a presence on the Internet these days. Each business or professional person should have a website with background information, product information, and contact information. This does not need to cost a bundle, either. There are web services that allow you set up you own site, even if you have little technical know-how, for less than fifty dollars and to maintain it for as little as ten dollars per month. One good site is **www. buildyoursite.com**, but there are many out there. Do your research and get yourself a website.

5. Maintain weak contacts. Once your site is up you can keep everyone in your contact base connected to you through e-mail and e-newsletters. This costs you nothing and allows people to follow your business and see new products or services immediately. You must always make a point to ask for e-mail addresses anytime you make a new contact.

6. Teach a class. Do you have an unusual skill or a hobby that you love? This doesn't have to be an academic endeavor. Many community colleges offer classes just for fun. These include gardening, photography, writing, basic automotive instruction, and even exercise classes. Instructing a class in any area exposes you to larger groups of people than you would meet on a daily basis. It also allows them a chance to get to know you and tell others about you and your business, even if it doesn't relate to the class you happen to be teaching.

7. Become involved in local government. Learn about your community and get involved. This can be through supporting nonprofit groups or serving on a city commission. This puts you in front of people and can provide you great local television or radio coverage. While it may not promote your business directly, it allows those in your community to become familiar with your face and name. It also sets you up as a leader in the mind of the public and someone whose opinion matters.

8. Contribute articles on your area of expertise to the local newspaper or to magazines. If your area is real estate investment, then you can do a series of articles or a column on the pitfalls and rewards of

111

that type of investment. If you are a plumber, you might consider some articles on ways the average homeowner can save money on their water bills and plumbing repairs. Use your imagination, and become an expert.

9. **Harness the power of the "blog."** Just like reality television has taken the country by storm, web logging, or "blogging," allows your network of people to keep up with you on a daily basis. They can follow along with your daily trek, celebrate your successes, and lament your failures. While you may think that you have nothing to offer and your life is just ordinary, you're wrong. We are a country that is absorbed in the minutia, if the long run of Seinfeld is any indication. We want to see others go through the typical ups and downs of everyday life and see how they deal with it. We want to relate to them and understand that those we admire and respect are human, just like we are. You can set up a blog for free through websites such as blogspot.com or livejournal.com and link those to your website. Each day your network of contacts can pull up your website, see what's new, and how your life is going today.

When you set up a blog there are several things you want to keep in mind.

a) Frequency is important, but don't be fanatical about it. Three times a week is fine; you don't have to post every day.

b) Pick a theme that will be helpful. Use your experiences, but try to find things to write about that will help others such as how to deal with rude people, how to improve your attitude, how to use your time wisely, and so on.

c) Ask a question. You want your blog to be as interactive as possible. Ask questions of people on your blog. Have you had a memorable family vacation this year? Or tell about a time you had to admit you were wrong. Let them come up with stories and ideas. This will add depth to your blog and make your readers feel like they are more closely connected to you.

d) Be cautious about personal information, and by "personal" I mean "private." While you want people to feel as though they know you, you also must remember that this is a public forum. Your posts will be read and talked about by those you know well and those you don't know well. While many people use a blog as their own personal diaries, I would strongly caution against this. Your closest family (spouse, children) may not appreciate having their private lives discussed with people they consider strangers. You must protect your private life but still make your blog personal and interesting. This is a balancing act, but it can be done and is very worthwhile - and it's practically FREE.

ASSEMBLE A GREAT TEAM

Probably everyone has heard that the greatest asset any business has is its people. That's not true. The greatest asset any business has is the RIGHT people performing the right jobs. As you travel along the path toward business and financial success, you will need to assemble your own team. This includes not only employees but also your team of advisors. Your "Board of Directors" should include your accountant, lawyer, and mentor(s).

In order to decide what qualities each of your team members should have, go back and look at the Person of Quality requirements. As you push yourself toward these goals, your team members should share these same core values and beliefs. I would be the first to tell you that it is not easy to determine what values someone has from a few interviews. Some people are very good at selling themselves in an interview. Let this be a warning. Someone who gives a great interview has probably had a lot of practice, while someone who is nervous and modest may have given very few. Think about this as you are talking to them. Ask them about the good results achieved in their previous jobs. Then ask them who was responsible for those results. Listen for the person who gives credit to others and promotes the team. Even when trying to get another job, most POQ's will credit past good results to the work of the group

113

rather than themselves. As you are interviewing, a good practice is to tell each potential member that there is a ninety-day probation period. Their reaction will give you some idea as to their work ethic. Do they respond like this is an unusual or unfair request, or do they take it as a challenge?

After working with someone for three months, you will have a good idea if he fits in with your POQ ideals or not. You will know individual work ethics and habits and be able to observe interactions with others. As always, if you find that you picked the wrong person then make the change immediately. Do not wait the full ninety days. Allow yourself to be wrong a few times, and be honest and upfront with those you have to replace. They will appreciate being told as quickly as possible that this job isn't working so they can move on to a better "fit."

When you think about choosing your advisory board of directors, you should go through a similar process. The one exception is that you do much more "up front" homework. You will want to ask others whom you know for referrals to good professional advisers and what experiences they have had with people you are interested in. The next step is to set up interviews with your potential advisors. Explain what you are looking for in an advisor and what your work goals are. Some professionals just like to do their jobs and no more, while others want to be involved in the goals and dreams of their clients. Listen carefully to what the person says and how he says it, and again look for the warning signs of a slick sales job. Remember, you do not want someone who tells you what to do and how to do it, you want someone who is willing to offer ideas and seek solutions.

As you bring on members of your team, you are looking for a synergy where two plus two equals … nine. Or even more. They must each complement each other. Where you have a weakness at least one of them must have strength. Assemble a team that can watch your back and compensate for any weak areas of the team as a whole. As you pull your team together, you must create an environment where all ideas are initially supported. This allows your members the freedom to offer unusual or untried solutions. The best way to do this is by asking questions. Allow the team to respond to each idea by giving the originator the chance to list all the good points of that particular solution first. Then give the nay-sayers their turn by allowing them to point out all the negative complications and possibilities next. Create a "Pros and Cons" sheet just like you do for your personal goals, and have your team discuss the possibilities. Do the pros outweigh the cons? Are there some good points we can take from this idea and combine with another idea to make a workable solution? As your team brainstorms possibilities from their assorted backgrounds and areas of specialty, you will come up with innovative and creative solutions you could have never dreamed up on your own.

115

"Unity is strength... when there is teamwork and collaboration, wonderful things can be achieved."

~ Mattie Stepanek ~

THE MILLIONAIRE GENIUS

~ *Notes* ~

~ Notes ~

~ *Notes* ~

CHAPTER SEVEN

SUPER MONEY

CHAPTER SEVEN

SUPER MONEY

120

Achieving a personal fortune is a beautiful thought. It's sad that people who work their whole lives so often end up with little or nothing to show for their efforts, and I know that you don't want to be one of those. Most of us spend time each day thinking about debts and bank balances, worrying about what we owe, and dreaming about what we would like to own. Unfortunately, most of us also lack a precise idea of our current financial position. If this sounds familiar, you are not alone. Financial planning is crucial because, just as with your personal goals, you can put off or ignore your financial goals.

Most parents want to teach their children responsibility, how to become self-sufficient and succeed in life. However, very few actually accomplish this task. Why? Because, as parents, we are limited to the experiences our parents passed on to us; they passed on the antiquated notion that "responsibility" is simply getting a job, saving a little money, and maybe purchasing a car or home. Hopefully, the following seven rules will open your eyes and help you avoid the traps that have stolen financial success from so many people.

WEALTH BUILDING RULE 1: GET OVER YOURSELF

Your biggest obstacle to attaining wealth is YOU. Too often people live their lives in a manner that is not conducive to creating riches and then get frustrated at "the system" when they only really have themselves to blame.

One of the most important financial decisions you will ever make is when to marry (or remarry) and then when to start a family. By putting off the walk down the aisle for a few years you can save a decade of frustration. Your first goal should be to become financially independent, with little or no debt, and have your investments in place. Once you have these three things, your odds of success are drastically improved by beginning your journey on a level playing field. After all, the number-one reason for divorce is financial trouble! So what do you do if you're already married and have a few kids? Keep reading.

WEALTH BUILDING RULE 2: DEBT IS A DISEASE

With a few notable exceptions, debt is a form of bondage, a disease that enslaves the borrower. A few years ago there was a young lady attending college who shot herself because she couldn't pay back $2,300 in credit card debt. Although an extreme example, it is a testament to the power money has over peoples' lives. Imagine your life without owing anyone anything, your car, your house, your education, all paid for in full. Do you like what you see? When you want it badly enough, you will make eliminating your debt a number one priority.

WEALTH BUILDING RULE 3: IF YOU DON'T LIKE WHERE YOUR PARENTS WERE AT YOUR AGE, DO THINGS DIFFERENTLY

The old cliché that "insanity is doing the same thing over and over again but expecting different results" holds just as true today as it did when it was originally written. If you don't like where your parents were at your age and you're doing the same things they were doing, stop it. During your childhood they taught you all they knew about money. For many people these early years established how they feel about their finances today. In order to become financially successful you must do something different than they did. Otherwise you will end up exactly as they are.

Wealth Building Rule 4: When You Begin a Job, Look at the Compensation of the Most Highly Paid Employee

Whether you are looking for employment now or are thinking about it sometime in the near future, one of the most important things for you to do is to look at what the top-dog gets at any company for which you are considering working. This will give you an idea of how high you can expect to climb in terms of earnings and promotion. If the CEO is making $30,000 a year, you have no chance to make six figures. Select a job accordingly.

Wealth Building Rule 5: Do Something You Love and Get Paid for It

I remember going to college and being surrounded with people who wanted to be artists, scientists, and businessmen, but instead they did what their parents or grandparents told them to do. There is no honor in being a doctor or a lawyer if you wake up every morning and hate your job. Pick a profession you love and have a passion for.

Wealth Building Rule 6: Understand the "Money Myth"

Money is nothing more than a piece of paper with the image of a long-dead person on it. When you understand that any power it has over you is derived from your relationship with it, you suddenly become free from the constant pressures and stress of thinking about it. Especially at times such as these, if you are putting money away for ten, fifteen, or twenty years down the road stop checking your portfolio every day! There is nothing you can gain from it except stress.

Wealth Building Rule 7: Your New Commodity is Not Your Labor, It's Your Ideas

With the advent of the Internet and other technological advances, you are no longer limited to supporting yourself or making a living by your physical labor. The only limit you have on yourself now is your own imagination; your ideas are your most valuable assets. Every man, woman, and child is a salesman; if you don't own a business or investments, then you sell your manual labor to a company in exchange for a paycheck. Change your product. The gap between the rich and poor does indeed grow larger with each passing year, but not because of inequalities or any other such injustices. Instead, it is because the rich understand money and how to use it. Capital is literally a seed; learn how to plant it to produce the best harvest. When you do this, you will rule your finances, not the other way around.

123

6 Simple Steps to Reduce Debt

Remember the Hustle? That's the dance craze that went out with leisure suits and Jerri Curl. Most people don't realize that they are still doing the Hustle; it's the Financial Hustle. They sit at the kitchen table each week staring at piles of bills. Which ones do we pay? Which can we put off a little longer? How can we keep this up?

Every family struggles with finances on occasion. The problem is that many people consistently stretch themselves to the limit of what they can afford. They commit every spare dime to payments on credit cards or to finance companies. With little or no savings, these families are living their lives waiting on the setback that will devastate them financially. It may be an illness, the loss of a job, a divorce, or any number of sudden emergencies that sets them on the path to ruin.

It's not so much that these individuals can't see the problem. The bills are staring them in the face every day and creating intense stress and anxiety. In fact, the picture is so bad that they can't see a solution. Every time I speak to an audience about investing my instinct tells me that I should focus my attention on debt. Most of the comments and e-mail

I receive are from individuals who are up to their eyeballs in debt and are ready to call it quits. Forget retirement. Forget saving for their kids' education. They're barely making ends meet, thanks to their monthly debt-servicing bill. They can't attempt to move forward until they remove themselves from the muck of debt that is dragging them down both emotionally and physically.

STEP 1: HOW MUCH DO YOU OWE? REALLY?

Do you even know? This is in some ways the most difficult step to take. It means facing the problem head on, something you have probably been trying to avoid doing for months. You have to draw up a simple personal budget setting out what income you have and what you are spending it on. There are two reasons for doing this. First, it tells you how big a problem you have. Second, it helps you check that you are not paying for things which you shouldn't be. Are there items on your credit card which you did not buy? Are the direct debits correct? Is anyone still collecting them when they should have stopped? These mistakes can and do happen, and they can be very expensive.

Most people never realize they're in trouble until they can't make all their minimum payments in a given month. That's not a situation you want to be faced with, so the first thing you've got to do is gather all your credit card, loans, and monthly statements. You need to list out the name of each card or bank, the interest rate charged, the outstanding loan amount, and the minimum monthly payment. List them in order of highest interest rate to lowest interest rate. Total up the total amount you owe and the minimum monthly payments. Don't worry about how much you owe. It's been said that almost anyone can eliminate their debts within five to seven years, including their mortgages.

STEP 2: STOP SPENDING!!!

The reason I make this step #2 is obvious. If you've done what you're supposed to do in step #1, you've had to come to terms with what your spending habits have done to your financial future. If you don't stop spending you'll just keep digging yourself deeper into debt, and one day you'll realize that you've been digging your own grave.

But don't let that total debt number get you down. The main thing is that you've realized that you've got to change something, and you've dedicated yourself to doing something about it. With the budget in front of you, now look at it carefully, calmly, and (above all) honestly. Try dividing your spending into three categories:

1. Spending which is fixed and cannot be reduced. Probably the only three in this category are mortgage interest payments, other loan repayments, and taxes.

2. Spending on essential items such as food, transport, gas, and utilities. Clearly you must spend on these items, but do you need to spend as much as you are doing at present? Are there any ways to reduce your energy costs? Carpool with co-workers? Take your lunch to work rather than eat out?

3. Non-essentials. This is where you have to be ruthless and make most of the cuts. Above all, this is where you have to be honest with yourself. Is going to the movies really necessary? Can you cut back or eliminate money spent on books and CDs? Do you really need a fancy cup of coffee every morning? Can you and your spouse eat dinner out once a month rather than once a week?

125

THE MILLIONAIRE GENIUS

You must resolve to use your credit card only for essentials from now on and pay the balance at the end of the month. If you're in the market for some big ticket item like a sofa or a TV, resolve to save up for that purchase rather than buy something you currently cannot afford. This is putting off gratification for the future reward that we've already talked about. And that reward is NO DEBT!

Step 3: What's Your Cash Flow?

This number is really important because you need to determine how much you can pay over and above the minimum required for all your debts. In the end it's up to you to decide how much of your extra cash flow will go toward debt repayment or investment. It all depends on what your goals are. My suggestion is to take a chunk of your extra cash (say around fifty to seventy percent of it) and put it toward debt repayment if your debt has truly become a burden to you.

Step 4: Build Your Emergency Fund

Before you invest or pay down any debt, check to see that you've set aside some money in an emergency fund. Three to six months' worth of after-tax living expenses in a money market account would be nice, but have a definite plan to continue to add money to your fund over the next three months or so. Remember that your return on your emergency fund is less important than the fact that you have the money set aside and readily available for unforeseen expenses.

I've read too many articles that suggest you should pay the minimum on your debts until you fully fund your emergency fund. I understand why this advice is given, but I think that if you've got one month's living expenses set aside you should do double duty - fund your emergency reserve and begin to pay more toward your debts. This way you'll have enough money set aside in your emergency fund after a period of a few months, and you'll have paid down some of that expensive debt.

Step 5: Consolidate/Transfer Debt

I'm betting you already know what I'm going to say, but I'll say it anyway. I'm sure you've had your mailbox filled with enticing offers from credit card companies offering some pretty attractive introductory rates for their cards. Maybe you got them from some of your current credit card companies and thought they were too good to pass up. We all get those zero-balance transfers for the next year or for the life of the loan. Perhaps those very offers are the ones that got you in trouble in the first place. Or maybe you're the type who endlessly transfers your balance from one card to the next in the hopes of escaping the interest monster. Now's the time to take advantage of those offers to find out the cost of the transfer and the length the interest rate will last.

Check the fine print of any offer you get to see if the fees for the transfers are worth it. Most companies will charge you either three percent of the balance transferred up to a maximum of forty to fifty dollars, with a minimum fee of five dollars.

Get a calculator and figure out if it makes sense to transfer your money. For instance, it makes no sense to transfer $2,000 from a 12% rate card to one offering 9% for six months. Why? You would be paying roughly one-hundred twenty dollars ($2,000 x 12% X .5 years) in interest over the next six months if you did nothing. If you transferred the balance, you would be paying a fifty-dollar fee (if the maximum were fifty) and interest of roughly eighty-two dollars ($2,050 x 8% x .5 years) for a total of $132 in fees and interest charged. So saving four percentage points didn't save you money, it actually cost you more money. Obviously the above example doesn't take into consideration that you would be making payments during the course of the six months, but that's why I called it simple math.

You should also look into consolidating your loans through refinancing your mortgage if you are able to do so. This will help you get a lower interest rate and give you the added bonus of making part of your payments tax-deductible. Just be careful not to continue spending because your cards are now "freed up." Put your credit cards on ice and keep only the two cards with the lowest fixed rate. After all you've been through, do you really want to fall back into the trap of frivolous spending and debt accumulation?

STEP 6: PAY OFF THE HIGHEST RATE CARD/LOAN FIRST

You should pay the minimum plus any additional funds you've earmarked for debt repayment against the highest interest rate card/loan and pay only the minimum on the other cards/loans. In other words, pay off your high interest rate cards first; then, when that's done, attack your next highest rate card/loan in the same manner. Why do it this way? Because this way guarantees that you pay the lowest total interest rate over the course of your DEBT REPAYMENT PLAN.

What about the method of debt repayment that a lot of gurus swear by, which involves paying all you can against the smallest debt, then working your way up the ladder to the largest debt? This technique is good for you psychologically but not so smart financially if that small loan balance doesn't carry the highest interest rate. Why? Because while your hard-earned dollars are paying off the loan with the smallest debt, there's another card or loan that's charging you more interest. If two cards have the same rate, put the additional money on the card with the smallest balance. This way it gets paid off faster, and you can transfer balances to it, or don't use it.

These are just a few ideas for of paying down your existing debts. While in some instances debt can be a good thing, too many people use debt in the wrong way. It's time you changed your spending habits in order to use debt properly. You must understand that debt is a form of leverage that has built countless fortunes for centuries, but if used improperly it has the ability to destroy your financial future. The main idea is to whittle your bad debt load down so that you can use the money you once were using for debt repayment and redirect it toward acquiring some real assets or building a business. That should be the reason for going through this debt repayment plan: funding your financial freedom plan.

WARNING!! DANGEROUS ROAD BLOCKS AHEAD!

There are several things to watch out for as you implement the new family budget:

a) Discouragement – It is easy to feel deprived and depressed when you have to do without certain things. Keep track of your family's progress by posting it in an area where all can view the results. Frequently talk about the progress made, and encourage one another to stay the course.

b) Legalism and inflexibility – The budget process is not designed to beat up on the family. Every budget must flex on occasion, and this is a good opportunity to discuss the problems and let everyone have input toward the solution.

c) Overcorrection – If the family falls back into old habits, revisit the commitment all the members made. Forgive each other, and try again. By consistently trying to work toward a goal the family does move forward, even if it is in small strides. And the lessons learned can have big payoffs down the road.

STRIVE FOR FINANCIAL LITERACY IN YOUR HOME

Read financial books, learn to understand bank and credit card statements, attend financial seminars, and talk to good financial planners. (You can e-mail me at **dave@millionairegenius.com** and I can recommend a few.) These steps can improve your understanding of what financial choices are the best ones for your family and which traps to avoid. This presents a challenge to most people who don't give their finances much thought on a daily basis. But this is your future. If you don't apply financial diligence, your life can spiral downward into a pit of debt and despair.

129

THE MILLIONAIRE GENIUS

BUDGET BUSTERS

Four things that can wreck even the best budget.

1. **Bookkeeping errors** – Keep your checkbook balanced and current, subtract automatic payments and ATMs, and appoint ONE bookkeeper per family.

2. **Hidden debts or expenses** – These include non-monthly expenses such as doctor bills, co pays, quarterly, semiannual, or annual insurance premiums. Be sure to set an allowance for these in the budget based on last year.

3. **Gifts** – Holidays and gift giving can be a major budget buster. Keep a calendar that anticipates your gift giving through the year and budget accordingly. Make a rule that no gifts are bought on credit.

4. **Impulse buying** – Everyone is guilty of this on occasion. Train yourself to view EVERY purchase in light of how it will affect your overall budget. Wait a minimum of thirty days before purchasing big ticket items and take the time to decide if you can afford it.

130

~ *Notes* ~

~ *Notes* ~

~ *Notes* ~

~ *Notes* ~

CHAPTER EIGHT

SUPER PERSISTENCE

CHAPTER EIGHT

SUPER PERSISTENCE

136

By definition, persistence is the ability to remain in an endeavor or action in spite of adverse conditions or occurrences. You have to ask yourself, how many times can you be knocked down and still get up and keep going? What is your limit? When will you call it quits? Have you given yourself a timeline in which you will try all this "goal" stuff and, if it doesn't work, go back to what you were already doing? Have you given yourself a worst-case scenario that will excuse you from trying anymore? Then you are giving yourself a reason to fail. You are hedging your bets rather than giving it one-hundred percent, and you know what? You're right. You will absolutely fail.

I have a writer friend who tells the following story of her career:

"I was a school teacher, and so was my husband. We had two young boys, and we struggled to make ends meet. I had always wanted to write a novel, and one day I decided to do it, hoping I could at least put some money away for the boys' college. I finished my first book in about a year and sent it out to every publisher in New York. Just as quickly they sent it right back. The rejections were harsh, and one even included a two-page, single-spaced letter from a leading editor about how bad it really was. It hurt terribly."

"Many times when I am depressed I go out to local cemetery and sit for a while because it is calm and serene. On this particular day I was walking amid the beautiful landscape and happened to see a large granite fruit bowl in the distance. I walked over and saw that this bowl was surrounded by benches, so I sat for a while and cried my

*eyes out, certain that every dream I had of being published
had been washed down the toilet. I looked down and on the
cement by my feet was the
word 'Triumph.'*

*"I thought it strange that there would be a word in the
cement and started looking around the bowl of fruit. Each
side of the bowl had a different word making up a single
sentence. That sentence was 'Triumph comes through
perseverance.' I decided right then that those publishers
in New York may never like one word that I write, but I
refused to give up and quit."*

137

She sold her next book and now, twenty-five years later, has
published more than twenty-six books and is a New York Times best-
selling author.

This is a good illustration of the fact that you can't pick a stopping
point before you start. You can't say, "I will try it for a year, and then I'll
let myself give up." You have to give it everything you have and determine
in your own mind that there is no going back.

When Hernando Cortez landed in Mexico in 1519 and faced a
much larger force of angry Aztecs, one of his lieutenants asked him if
they should retreat to their ships. Instead Cortez said, "Burn them."

In your own life you must determine to burn your lifeboats. If
you do not give yourself the opportunity to quit then you will be forced
to move forward. Look back at what you wrote down as your One
Motivating Desire. Was it providing a better life for your children, or
maybe giving yourself the freedom from the corporate rat race? Many
of you have probably seen or heard about people who survive incredible
hardships. From accidents to days or weeks on the open ocean, some
people have the ability to survive against mind-boggling odds. How do
they do it? What separates them from "normal people" who would die
very quickly? The answer is that most of them have a very strong will
to live. They have that one motivating desire that will overcome every
hardship they encounter.

You can do this with your own goals. While they may not be life and death, they are your future and represent the life you want. When you come upon hard times or face what may seem to be insurmountable obstacles, focusing on this one desire will get you through. And reminding yourself of what you are doing and how to do it will set you on the path to success again.

If you should get depressed and dejected and feel like you just can't move forward, there is something you can do about it. I have developed a short list of questions that contain some of the major ideas in this book. At any time, you can turn to this list and ask yourself these questions and find your path once again.

> *"Flaming enthusiasm, backed up by horse sense and persistence, is the quality that most frequently makes for success."*
> ~ Dale Carnegie ~

MY ONE MOTIVATING DESIRE

ATTITUDE

1. Have you allowed your internal critic to bombard you with negative thoughts? List these. Then draw a line through those negative thoughts and replace them with positive thoughts.

2. Has destructive Internal Dialogue convinced you that you can't move forward? Why? Write down what you think is stopping you, and then list possible solutions.

3. Are there still some life events or issues from the past that you are allowing to hold you back? List these. Now resolve to take control and let them go. Stop using the past as an excuse to delay your future success.

4. Are you allowing your own limitations of what you think you can achieve to slow down or stop your progress? Resolve to take responsibility for this behavior and list at least three things you will do to move past your own preconceived ideas.

5. Are you beating yourself up for a failure? STOP! Remember that there will always be some failures, but those people who succeed push through those failures to reach their goals. Write down whatever failure you are feeling bad about. Once you have written it down, resolve to forgive yourself and let it go.

6. Have you faced a crisis that has stopped you in your tracks? Write it down. Now review the tools in your Crisis Kit. List three actions you will take to move past this crisis or diminish its effects on your goals.

7. Are you putting the Person of Quality attributes into action each day? Which ones are you struggling with? List them here. What actions will you take to incorporate these into your daily life?

8. Has your POQ plan jumped off track? Answer yes or no to the following questions:

a) Are you confronting reality? _____

b) Have you removed the negative? _____

c) Are you focusing on your plan? _____

d) Are you leading a disciplined lifestyle? _____

If you answered "No" to any of the above questions, then explain why: _____

What actions will you take this week to correct these issues?

_____

1. Are you reassessing and refining your goals as you go? If you answered no, explain why. _____

Resolve to review the chapter on goal setting and see where the problems lie. Have you set your goals too low and become bored with them? Have you not set good short-term goals and tasks and been overwhelmed by the long-term goals? If you haven't yet set good, definable long-term and short-term goals, it's not too late. Do that now. Forgive yourself and move on, don't beat yourself up.

2. Have you received some feedback or criticism that has stalled your progress? What was it? Write it here, and then list three things you will do to overcome that mindset.

3. Have you contacted a mentor? List his/her name here.

_____

If you haven't, why not? What is stopping you? List the reason.

_____

_____

_____

Are you letting fear or uncertainty get the best of you? Is that how you want to live your life? Go back and focus on your One Motivating Desire. Now List the actions you will take to find and meet a mentor. _____

_____

_____

_____

141

THE FIVE MOST EXPENSIVE WORDS

There are certain words which should be deleted from the vocabulary of each person interested in success. Avoid these words like the plague. These five words, when used on the tongue or practiced in anyway in one's behavior, are the surest way to mediocrity at best and poverty at worst.

1. CAN'T

Very little in life "can't" be done. "Can't" means "Won't." If you honestly believe that your current results are the best you can expect, then you are probably right. Why is it, though, that a relative newcomer can occupy a desk right next to yours, sell exactly the same product or service as you, and break all the office sales records? Why do some people earn $22,000 a year while someone just a few desks away earns $222,000?

Much of it has to do with whether they accept the weak-minded philosophy of "can't."

Why not look at challenging situations with the view to solving the problem rather than being swamped by it? There is ALWAYS a solution. I'm always only one idea away from solving whatever obstacle is in my path.

"CAN" is my motto. I might not know how, but I believe that something can be done. My job is to believe that solutions come to those who refuse to be the victim of circumstances.

2. BLAME

If you choose to get involved in blaming others for your troubles, your future is indeed dim. There is no way to succeed if you are constantly pointing your fingers to others as the cause of what is going on in your life.

Understand that if you are to succeed then you must accept total responsibility for your life. The sales you make, the attitude you have, and the emotional state you find yourself in are, in one form or another, due to some choices you have made. Your results have little to do with how your company or your business is managed. Your sales are not low because of the economy or the government or your wife. It has to do with you and with you only. Take responsibility for your life. Never point the finger at someone else.

> *"People blame their environment. There is only one person to blame – and only one – themselves."*
> ~ Robert Collier ~

3. PASSIVE

I have been working with high achievers for years. I've heard and seen enough of them to know, without a doubt, that the difference between the achievers and the non-achievers is that non-achievers leave so much of their business to chance and luck. I call it the "Hope and Pray" technique of success. They hope and pray for sales but wait passively for the phone to ring. They hope and pray for money but do nothing to get it flowing. They hope and pray that the manager will get off their back, but they refuse to move into action, hoping instead things will get better all on their own.

I've never seen the phone ring all by itself, nor have I seen significant ventures built, nor significant increases in income, without people deciding what they want changed, developing a plan to change it, moving into action, and being held accountable for the success. Rather, what I so often see is people accepting the status quo and not actively pursuing the keys to success.

Why do retail establishments wait passively for customers to walk in? Why wouldn't they create effective marketing campaigns to attract people? Why wouldn't they do a cross-marketing campaign with the shop next door and sell each other's services? Why wouldn't they create some compelling reasons for people to move into action? If they offered some special deal, put a deadline on it, and created some life around their establishment, wouldn't they be better off than sitting in their stores waiting for business to come to them?

If you move into action, provide irresistible offers, compelling reasons to call you, and provide awesome service, I promise you that you will gain the success that you strive for.

143

4. Conformity

Reluctance to try different things is a problem I see many people struggling with. In sales, for example, most methods of prospecting were developed in the 1950's, and little has changed since then for most people. We have been told that prospecting is a function of rejection. If you knock on enough doors you will make a certain number of sales.

I advocate breaking away from everyone else's stale sales techniques and selling without rejection. I'm all for creating systems to attract more leads than you know what to do with. How different would your attitude and motivation be if you went to work tomorrow morning knowing that you had 300 qualified leads from people who were predisposed to buy what you sell?

So much activity today is based on the dangerous word "conformity." People follow the crowd. I call it the herd mentality. If the masses are doing one thing, I recommend doing the exact opposite. If nobody in your industry has a marketing package, you be the first. Break the mould! Change the norm! Try something no one else is doing! Let's face it, the masses are usually wrong, especially about earning money. What the world needs are success-minded individuals who are willing to challenge the status-quo.

5. Quit

If a light came on in your car which indicated there were problems with your engine, you would think a person insane if he took out a hammer and smashed the light. Sure the light would go off, but that would not do anything to relieve the problem with the engine.

The same applies to you. The real reason that you are not reaching your goals is YOU. Taking a hammer to the red light (your company, your boss) will not solve your basic problem. You must address the issue of changing yourself and your mind first, then success will follow.

~ Notes ~

~ *Notes* ~

~ Notes ~

~ *Notes* ~

CHAPTER NINE

SUPER SATISFACTION

CHAPTER NINE

SUPER SATISFACTION

150

As you go through your plan you will reach the goals you set one by one. And you will set new goals and strive toward them as well. So when do you know that you've made it? This is different for every individual. Some have a set goal or amount of money or time frame that they pursue; others leave it open-ended and just follow their instinct. When you do, be sure to take a deep breath and proclaim, "I've Arrived!"

I think that you will reach a satisfied and fulfilling life much sooner than you realize once you start on your own path to success. Few realize that success isn't a thing, it's an emotion or feeling. We feel successful, therefore we are. There are people who are perfectly content and happy working the jobs that they have, raising their children and spending time with family. There is no rule that says you have to be dissatisfied with these elements of your life in order to pursue long-term goals. This is merely a starting point. You can always improve, but the path to success isn't about getting there. It's about the journey. What do you find out about yourself and others as you go? What lessons did you learn and want to share with those who may one day approach you and ask you to be their mentor?

Part of a successful attitude and lifestyle is the ability to give back. Reach out to your community, to your family, and to others who seek to learn what you know. As you achieve greater and greater heights you may notice that the goals that you set have more to do with moving others forward rather than yourself. This is a natural result of living the Person of Quality lifestyle. It becomes second nature to lift others up and help them find their way. You honor those who helped you by concentrating your efforts on those whom you can now help.

I'll leave you with a few final thoughts to set you on your way to success.

I HAVE WHAT IT TAKES

Repeat these words to yourself until you believe them. Type them up and hang them on your refrigerator, wall, or computer. Look at them each day and believe in yourself.

Embrace the changes in your life with an attitude of joy and contentment. Convince yourself that you can and will do whatever it takes to meet your goals and live the life you dream for yourself.

Be patient. Change doesn't happen overnight and will take time. Don't rush through your plan. You will end up skipping steps and becoming frustrated. Remember that this is about the journey. You don't get to the top of the mountain in one day; you get there step-by-step with dogged persistence.

Take time to appreciate who you are right now and who you want to become. Someday you will look back and be very proud of the decisions that you are making today and the changes you are implementing.

Learn to listen and think before you speak. A big part of learning is to be quiet and let others teach you. You will never know what you miss by talking. Others have valid input that can help you, and they want to help you. Let them.

Don't fear change or uncertainty. We usually are most apprehensive about those things for which we don't have definite outcomes or solutions already in mind. Believe that you have the ability to solve any problem that will come, and don't imagine monsters in the closet. Get the facts, do your homework, and boldly move forward. You mustn't let the risk of failure keep you from the glorious rewards that await you.

151

THE MILLIONAIRE GENIUS

YOU CAN HAVE MORE
AND BE MORE
BY DOING MORE!

The next step is yours!

WWW.MILLIONAIREGENIUS.COM

"*You can have peace of mind, improved health and an ever-increasing flow of energy. Life can be full of joy and satisfaction.*"

~ Norman Vincent Peale ~

153

THE MILLIONAIRE GENIUS

ABOUT DAVID OGUNNAIKE

David Ogunnaike is founder of "THE ONE DREAM TEAM" in Toronto, Canada, the fastest growing personal development networking team in North America.

David Ogunnaike is considered to be one of North America's most exciting presenters. He has worked with and shared the stage with some of the top authors and speakers in the world including: Bob Proctor, Robert Kiyosaki, Robert Allen, Dexter Yager and Gerry Robert.

David's high-energy, 'cut-to-the-chase' style keeps his audience spellbound. He teaches using unique techniques and high involvement so that participants learn faster, remember more and achieve maximum results. The change in people is long lasting and immediate. David Ogunnaike's motto is "talk is cheap" and his unique ability is getting people to take "action" in the real world to produce real success.

Over 100,000 participants have attended David Ogunnaike seminars. He has Transformed people's lives!

Want More Income?

David Ogunnaike regularly partners with individuals to create multiple sources of income. If you are serious about achieving a higher income and more time freedom, then apply today to join Super Dave's team.

(Several opportunities available; joint venture's, licenses, partnerships, franchises, speaking, training, publishing.)

Call 1-(416) 831-1420
or send an email to:
Dave@MillionaireGenius.com

SHARE THIS MESSAGE

Bulk Discounts
Discounts start at a low number of copies, ranging from 30% to 50% off based on the quantity chosen.

Custom Publishing
Would you like a private label? or a customization to suit your needs. We could even highlight specific chapters.

Sponsorship
Would you like to sponsor this book? It's a great way to advertise your product or service in a unique way!

Dynamic Speakers
Authors are available to you, to share their expertise at your event!

Call LifeSuccess Publishing at 1-800-473-7134 or email
info@lifesuccesspublishing.com for more information

You Were Born Rich

Bob Proctor
ISBN # 978-0-9656264-1-5

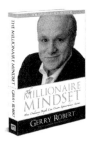

The Millionaire Mindset
*How Ordinary People Can
Create Extraordinary Income*

Gerry Robert
ISBN # 978-1-59930-030-6

Rekindle The Magic In
Your Relationship
Making Love Work

Anita Jackson
ISBN # 978-1-59930-041-2

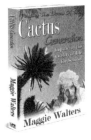

Finding The Bloom of
The Cactus Generation
*Improving the quality of
life for Seniors*

Maggie Walters
ISBN # 978-1-59930-011-5

The Beverly Hills Shape
The Truth About Plastic Surgery

Dr. Stuart Linder
ISBN # 978-1-59930-049-8

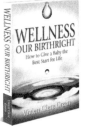

Wellness Our Birthright
*How to give a baby the best
start in life.*

Vivien Clere Green
ISBN # 978-1-59930-020-7

Lighten Your Load

Peter Field
ISBN # 978-1-59930-000-9

Change & How To
Survive In The New
Economy
*7 steps to finding freedom
& escaping the rat race*

Barrie Day
ISBN # 978-1-59930-015-3

Other books from LifeSuccess Publishing

Stop Singing The Blues
*10 Powerful Strategies For
Hitting The High Notes In
Your Life*

Dr. Cynthia Barnett
ISBN # 978-1-59930-022-1

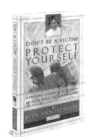

Don't Be A Victim,
Protect Yourself
*Everything Seniors Need To
Know To Avoid Being Taken
Financially*

Jean Ann Dorrell
ISBN # 978-1-59930-024-5

A "Hand Up", not a
"Hand Out"
*The best ways to help others
help themselves*

David Butler
ISBN # 978-1-59930-071-9

Doctor Your Medicine Is
Killing Me!
*One Mans Journey From
Near Death to Health and
Wellness*

Pete Coussa
ISBN # 978-1-59930-047-4

I Believe in Me
*7 Ways for Woman to Step
Ahead in Confidence*

Lisa Gorman
ISBN # 978-1-59930-069-6

The Color of Success
*Why Color Matters in your
Life, your Love, your Lexus*

Mary Ellen Lapp
ISBN # 978-1-59930-078-8

If Not Now, When?
What's Your Dream?

Cindy Nielsen
ISBN # 978-1-59930-073-3

The Skills to Pay the
Bills… and then some!
*How to inspire everyone in
your organisation into high
performance!*

Buki Mosaku
ISBN # 978-1-59930-058-0

OTHER BOOKS FROM LIFESUCCESS PUBLISHING

The Secret To Cracking
The Property Code
*7 Timeless Principles for
Successful Real Estate
Investment*

Richard S.G. Poole
ISBN # 978-1-59930-063-4

Why My Mother Didn't
Want Me To Be Psychic
*The Intelligent Guide To The
Sixth Sense*

Heidi Sawyer
ISBN # 978-1-59930-052-8

The Make It Happen Man
*10 ways to turn obstacles
into stepping stones without
breaking a sweat*

Dean Storer
ISBN # 978-1-59930-077-1

Change your body
Change your life
*with the Fittest Couple in
the World*

Matt Thom &
Monica Wright
ISBN # 978-1-59930-065-8

Good Vibrations!
*Can you tune in to a more
positive life?*

Clare Tonkin
ISBN # 978-1-59930-064-1

The Millionaire Genius
*How to wake up the money
magic within you.*

David Ogunnaike
ISBN # 978-1-59930-026-9

Scoring Eagles
*Improve Your Score In Golf,
Business and Life*

Max Carbone
ISBN # 978-1-59930-045-0

The Einstein Complex
*Awaken your inner genius,
live your dream.*

Dr. Roger A. Boger
ISBN # 978-1-59930-055-9